DR STEFAN BUCZACKI'S GARDENING HINTS

Stefan Buczacki is one of Britain's leading gardening experts. Although probably best known for his appearances on Radio Four's *Gardeners' Question Time*, he is also a highly respected television presenter on such programmes as *Gardeners' World* (BBC2), his own series *That's Gardening* (TVS) and the daytime magazine *Bazaar* (BBC1). He also writes and presents the popular radio series *The Gardening Quiz* and contributes to a wide range of magazines and newspapers. For many years he was engaged in horticultural research and gained international recognition in this field.

Dr Buczacki has written numerous successful books on such topics as Victorian flower gardening, gardening for beginners, garden ecology and the scientific principles of gardening, as well as the standard reference work on garden pests and diseases and *The Essential Gardener*, a comprehensive guide to successful modern gardening. He is married with two sons and lives near Stratford-upon-Avon.

DR STEFAN BUCZACKI'S
Gardening Hints

PAN BOOKS
LONDON, SYDNEY AND AUCKLAND

First published in 1992 by Pan Books Limited,
a division of Pan Macmillan Publishers Limited
Cavaye Place London SW10 9PG

1 2 3 4 5 6 7 8 9

© Dr Stefan Buczacki 1992

The right of Dr Stefan Buczacki to be identified as
author of this work has been asserted by him
in accordance with the Copyright, Designs and
Patents Act 1988.

ISBN 0 330 32259 1

Photoset by Parker Typesetting Service, Leicester
Printed and bound in Great Britain by
Richard Clay Ltd, Bungay, Suffolk

Contents

DR STEFAN BUCZACKI'S GARDENING HINTS

1

Introduction and general hints

Gardening never ceases to amaze me. Even after so many seasons with my hands in the soil and so many years with *Gardeners' Question Time*, I am sure that I still learn something new every week. For gardening knowledge is acquired in a multitude of different ways. Early on, we absorb vast helpings of information from our first gardening books. Then we watch more experienced gardeners in action, follow radio and television programmes and dip into more serious gardening tomes. But I am increasingly convinced that the difference between the good gardener and the merely average is to be measured not in their overall knowledge but in the little nuggets of practical information they have accumulated. These form the icing on the cake of basic know-how. They transform the theorist into the accomplished practitioner and while there is no absolute substitute for experience, the next best thing is to acquire your practical nuggets from someone who has made it his business to collect them.

The gardening hints in this book have all been verified in my own garden – so they have worked for at least one gardener already. I have acquired them through a wide variety of means. Some I came across originally in old gardening books and then tried and perhaps adapted them to my own purposes. Many ideas and techniques have arisen quite by chance in the course of my own gardening activities and must be, I assume, original. Yet others have been picked up from professional colleagues and the numerous and wonderfully knowledgeable amateur gardeners whom I have had the pleasure of meeting over the years. Unfortunately, I have no records of all those who have unwittingly contributed to my own fund of knowledge and so I can only thank them collectively – and hope that a few will recognize their own hints now being put to good and wider use.

When I first began to write the book, I realized that to try to produce, let's say, one hundred hints in each of a number of sections (vegetables, fruit, pests and so on) wouldn't be feasible. Inevitably, some of the sections are larger than others and of course some of the hints are applicable to more than one category, but in general I think you will find the system works pretty well and the information is accessible.

If you find my hints useful, I do hope you will write and say so; and in fact I hope you will also say if you try any and find they don't work. But I hope most of all that if you have hints of your own, you will let me know. Perhaps, if I can accumulate enough, there might be a follow-up volume! After all, so much of gardening is about sharing – sharing plants, and sharing experiences.

Friendship gardening

Gardening is about friendships, shared delights and shared problems. Discuss your garden with friends and neighbours; invite them to see your garden and I am sure they will reciprocate; and, above all, swap plants with them.

A token of your esteem

Buy Horticultural Trades Association gift tokens for gardening friends and relatives.

Visit gardens

If you enjoy visiting gardens, join the National Trust and the Royal Horticultural Society, who between them account for a fair proportion of the finest gardens in the country – and what better idea than membership of these organisations as a present for a gardening friend?

Treat yourself in the spring to a copy of *The Yellow Book* of gardens open to the public: not only will this guarantee you some enjoyable visits but you will learn a great deal of good gardening too.

Well-spent evenings

Support your local colleges and learn a great deal about gardening by attending evening classes.

Bend an ear

Listen to *Gardeners' Question Time* every week!

Seed catalogues

Send away for as many seed catalogues as possible each year. Not only will you then see the full range of varieties available, but also the catalogues represent the best free source of gardening advice.

You and your garden centre

Talk to your local garden centre: tell them the types of plants you want them to sell, let them know of your problems – and encourage them to join the Garden Centres Association.

Remember that a good garden centre will replace any hardy perennial plant that fails within twelve months so long as it has been given appropriate care.

Planning for autumn

At the height of summer, go round the garden with a notebook and record those plants that need moving or dividing – it will be impossible to remember when autumn comes.

Leave wild plants alone!

Never dig up plants from the wild for your garden. Not only is this illegal, it is also unnecessary since seed of all wild species is now readily available.

No illegal immigrants

Do not bring home plants or plant material from holidays abroad until you have read the Ministry of Agriculture regulations on the subject.

Using chemicals

Never use a garden chemical for any purpose other than that stated on the label – you could be breaking the law if you do.

Good neighbours

Be sure when planting trees or other large plants in your garden that they don't adversely affect your neighbour's house or view.

Shelter in the north

Don't be afraid to place fairly tender plants against a north-facing wall. In practice, they will be sheltered there from the rapid thawing that so often causes damage to fragile tissues.

Danger from the east

Do not position your more tender plants in an east-facing situation: the early morning sun in winter will thaw out frozen tissues very rapidly, so causing them damage.

Temperature drops

On average, the temperature falls 1°F for every 100 ft rise in contour (or approximately 0.5°C for every 30 m).

Ominous spot

Never put a new plant in exactly the same position as that in which one of the same or a related type has died.

Larger than life

Treat yourself to a small hand magnifier, giving an enlargement of about ten times. Not only will it enable you to see greenfly larger than life, but it will open up a fascinating and beautiful new microscopic world in your garden.

2

Design and maintenance

Planning a new garden

When planning a new garden, go to the highest vantage point (usually a bedroom window) and make a sketch plan, noting the position of shady and sunny spots. Then, when working out the design in detail, remember that fruit, vegetables, pools and greenhouses are those features most in need of sun.

Optical illusions

To make a garden appear larger than it really is, keep the centre fairly free from plants, try to arrange shrubs so that they obscure the boundaries and introduce twists and turns into the design to give a hint of mystery.

If possible, place a focal point such as a striking shrub or an ornament where it can be glimpsed through an archway – this helps to take the eye a long way and make the garden seem larger.

Adding interest

To increase the interest of your garden design, as well as provide additional support for climbing plants and help to separate discrete areas, try placing one or two rustic archways over bends and curves in your paths.

Lights at night

To bring your garden to life in the evening, why not install low-voltage garden lighting? For a very modest outlay, you can obtain spike- or umbrella-pattern lamps to place among plants or, as a safety feature, by paths and steps; and they can all be run via a small plug transformer off a supply taken from a convenient socket in the house.

Avoiding frost pockets

In a sloping garden, cold air may accumulate because, being denser than warm air, it rolls downhill. Simply making a gap in a hedge or fence on the down slope side may allow the air to continue downhill, relieve the garden of a frost pocket and so permit the more successful growing of a wide variety of plants.

Plants for shady corners

To bring interest all year round to difficult, damp and shady parts of the garden, grow a range of evergreen hardy ferns, including *Phyllitis scolopendrium* (the hart's tongue), *Blechnum penna-marina* and *Polystichum setiferum* 'Divisilobum'.

Ornamental vegetables

If the idea of a vegetable plot strikes you as uninteresting, why not incorporate vegetables among ornamental plants? Some of them (lettuces, beetroot and carrots especially) can be most attractive in their own right.

A children's garden

For a children's garden, choose the part of the garden with the best soil and the best growing conditions – nothing will deter young gardeners as much as having to struggle against the elements.

Sizing a patio

When constructing a patio, be sure that it is big enough for the purpose intended. Before starting work, set out a table and chairs – and then draw the chairs back from the table. It is surprising how much additional room is needed to do this comfortably.

Retaining wall

When building a garden retaining wall, slope the wall slightly into the soil bank to make it more stable.

How to train climbers

The strongest and most versatile method of training climbing plants against walls is to use vine eyes or eyed bolts to which strong training wire has been attached.

Fixing trellis

When fixing trellis to a wall, use battens to raise it from the surface. This permits the free flow of air round climbing plants and lessens the problems from mildew and other diseases.

Facing the front

Keep your front garden simple; it is the face of your garden that passers by will see and the simpler it is, the easier it will be to keep neat and tidy.

Make your ornaments mossy

Use milk and/or soft cow manure to paint garden ornaments and so encourage the growth of lichens, moss and algae.

Clean your canes

Clean garden canes after use by allowing them to dry, then drop their ends on to a hard surface to knock out the plug of soil from the base. Finally dip them in proprietary disinfectant and rinse them in clean water before storing them.

Autumn clear-out

When clearing up autumn leaves, don't forget those in drains and gutters.

Care with creosote

Take care not to splash creosote on to plants when treating garden woodwork as it can cause very severe leaf scorching.

Moving soil

When planning to move soil, remember that a cubic metre (yard) weighs a tonne (2000 lbs) – so budget your time and energy accordingly.

A quick way to tidy the garden

If time is really precious and the garden is looking unkempt, spend what few moments you have mowing the lawn – nothing makes the whole look as instantly tidy. And if time is truly desperate, simply edge the lawn rather than mow it.

3

Soil care

How to determine texture

Rub a sample of soil between moistened fingers (spit on them) to gain an indication of its texture – a sandy soil feels rough, a clay soil greasy and a loam somewhere in between. An expert can fairly accurately determine the percentage of clay in a soil by this simple test.

Improving clay soil

Improve a clay soil by double digging, little by little, and incorporating masses of organic matter – it is the *only* reliable way.

What's your pH?

You will get an indication of the pH of your garden soil by looking at the wild plants growing nearby – for instance, rhododendrons indicate high acidity and clematis (old man's beard) high alkalinity.

Increasing acidity

The only reliable way to increase the acidity of a naturally alkaline soil is by adding sulphur; peat will not make any difference unless added in unrealistically large quantities. Check with the manufacturer's directions for the amounts of sulphur required on different types of soil.

Is your lime necessary?

Never add lime to the garden without first checking the soil's pH to see if it is really needed.

The best lime

The best and safest type of lime to apply to garden soils is ground limestone or 'garden lime'; and the best time to apply it is in the autumn.

Don't lime when you manure

Never apply lime and manure to the soil at the same time because they will react together to produce harmful ammonia. Allow at least two months to elapse between the two operations.

Nutrient deficiency

Don't rely on kits sold to test soil nutrient content. Most are very unreliable, especially for the measurement of nitrogen. If, instead, you base your plant-feeding on using balanced fertilizers each season, deficiencies of individual nutrients are unlikely to arise.

Iron deficiency

Dark green leaf veins combined with abnormally yellowed foliage is a symptom of iron deficiency, especially significant on chalky soils and corrected by application of sequestered iron.

Bonemeal or steamed boneflour?

Don't confuse steamed boneflour with bonemeal: the former is more finely ground and contains quicker-acting phosphates, but the valuable small amount of nitrogen present in bonemeal is almost all removed by the steaming process.

Autumn digging

When digging the soil in autumn, don't make the mistake of breaking down the clods too much for the winter rains will then only form a compacted surface. Leave the clods rough for nature to disintegrate slowly.

The right way with a fork

Never force a fork – if there is serious resistance when you are attempting to dig up a plant, stop before you bend or snap the tines. Dig round with a spade to form a small trench and so expose more of the root system this way before proceeding.

The right way with a spade

Always push a spade into the ground with the ball of your foot, not with the instep; and whenever possible use leather boots, not wellingtons, for digging.

4

Fertilizers and feeding

The best ash

While ash from a bonfire of twigs and branches is of
some value as a fertilizer for the potash that it contains,
ash from the domestic grate is much less useful: coal ash
has almost no potash while even the ash from logs,
being largely heartwood, is fairly low in potash content.

Don't hoard manure

Do not stack manure for more than a year before use
because a large proportion of the nutrients will by then
have been leached out.

Gardening co-op

You will save money by clubbing together with gardening friends to buy fertilizers and composts in bulk; but
never do this with pesticides as it is illegal to split up
large quantities and use them in any other than the
original container.

Fertilizer dosage

To convert general fertilizer doses from those given in reference books, the rates given for blood, fish and bone should be reduced by one quarter if you use Growmore and multiplied by 20 if you rely solely on manure or compost. These calculations will give you equivalent amounts of nitrogen although the *proportions* of nitrogen, phosphate and potash differ between the three.

Use a set of scales to determine how much of each of your various types of fertilizer can be held in one of your gloved hands, then you can convert the doses given in gardening books to handfuls.

Powdered fertilizers

When applying fertilizer powder, always break up any lumps that may have formed in order to obtain an even distribution – but use gloves, not bare hands, to do this.

Small quantities of fertilizer may be spread more uniformly if they are mixed with fine dry sand.

After sprinkling fertilizer around plants, always rake or hoe it into the surface or it will cake.

If rain doesn't fall within forty-eight hours of applying a powdered fertilizer to your lawn, use a hosepipe to wash it in.

Don't allow fertilizers of different type to come into contact with each other as may happen if they are stored in packets or paper bags in direct contact. They may interact chemically.

Compost for azaleas

Don't use animal manures for rhododendrons and azaleas: vegetable composts are much more satisfactory.

Transplant shock

When transplanting, water in the young plants with a solution of liquid fertilizer rather than plain water to help them regenerate their roots and overcome the transplanting shock.

It is always worth giving a foliar feed with liquid fertilizer to any plant that has suffered some form of shock or check to its growth; this will encourage it to overcome the damage.

Beware of bogus manure

When buying farmyard manure in small quantities in bags, check carefully that you are not simply buying a bag of straw with a little manure on top – the weight usually gives the game away.

When to use peat

Only use peat in the garden where its unique property of high acidity is needed. For other purposes, use different types of organic matter derived from renewable sources.

Liquid or solid?

Use a liquid fertilizer to obtain the most rapid results in the summer on fast-growing plants; at the beginning and end of the season, a solid fertilizer is more beneficial.

Potash for flowering

To encourage an ornamental plant to flower, try giving it liquid tomato fertilizer, which is high in potash, once a fortnight during the summer months.

Don't overdose annuals

Be cautious in applying fertilizer to summer-flowering annuals as it is very easy to give them too much and so encourage leaves rather than flowers.

Variegated means more care

Plants with variegated foliage usually need a little more feeding and better growing conditions than their plain-leaved relatives: they contain less chlorophyll and are therefore less effective at manufacturing their own food by photosynthesis.

Bulbs

As the flowers fade on bulbs, cut off the dead heads and give liquid fertilizer to the foliage, but do not cut them down completely until six weeks after the end of flowering.

Is it organic?

If you are an avowedly organic gardener, choose carefully when buying blood, fish and bone fertilizer. Many commercial brands are in fact only organically *based*, having had sulphate of potash added to compensate for the natural deficiency of potash in the unamended mixture.

Vegetables

When giving fertilizer to your vegetables, don't apply it all at once. Rake one third of the allotted dose into the bed about one week before sowing, a second third about two weeks after the plants have emerged or been planted, and the final third when they are approximately half grown.

When applying fertilizer to vegetable crops, scatter it along the sides of the rows rather than over the centre – this will enable it more readily to be washed down to reach the actively growing feeder roots.

Shrubs

Apply general fertilizer to roses and other shrubs immediately after pruning.

5

Compost

Home-made compost bin

You can construct a strong, well-ventilated compost bin from four second-hand wooden pallets, screwed together and treated with preservative.

Starting a new heap

When starting a new compost heap or bin, use a few forkfuls of compost from the base of the old pile – this will contain worms and micro-organisms to start the new process more efficiently.

Cover your heap

Use hessian or plastic netting to cover the compost heap – it will allow some rain to penetrate and prevent the heap from drying out but not so much that it will become sodden.

Use two bins

Use a double compost bin for ease of management – you can be filling one bin while the second supplies rotted compost.

Accelerator

Apply a scattering of compost accelerator or other nitrogen source after every 20 cm (8 in) or so of debris have been added to a compost bin.

Ventilate your compost

Always provide some aeration to a compost heap or bin: waterlogging, poor drainage and ventilation are the commonest reasons for a failure to make good compost.

If you have a compost shredder, prepare a stack of chopped woody material during the winter and add it little by little to the heap during the summer to ameliorate the effect of masses of grass cuttings.

Mower-cum-shredder

If you don't have a compost shredder, modest quantities of twigs and other small, woody matter can be chopped very effectively by spreading them on an area of rough lawn and collecting them with a robust rotary mower.

Don't shred newspaper

Don't be tempted to try shredding newspaper in a compost shredder: even the most powerful machine will shred paper very slowly and laboriously and can easily be blocked by it. Paper shredded into thin strips by an office shredder will rot down very effectively however.

Keep out of compost

Compost all organic waste except bones, chicken carcasses and other animal scraps from the kitchen, and also avoid composting brassica plants affected with clubroot and onion plants affected with white rot.

Leaf mould cage

Use four posts and chicken wire to construct a leaf mould cage of about 1 m (3 ft) cube; leaves rot down more slowly than other garden debris, and if added to the compost heap they may block it. Jump on the leaves to compress them. After about 18 months you will have a rich mulch.

Don't add lime

Unless you garden on a very acid soil and all of your garden refuse is from acid-loving plants, you should never find it necessary to add lime to the compost heap.

Potato blight

Never tip old potato tubers on to the top of a compost heap, always cover them with other debris. If any bearing the blight fungus are left on the surface, they may subsequently produce diseased sprouts bearing spores that will infect the new season's crop.

Surviving seeds

The only seeds I have found that will normally survive the composting process are tomatoes.

Benevolent mould

If you find whitish mould growth in your compost or mulch, don't worry. It will not be honey fungus or some other harmful organism but simply the microscopic fungi that help bring about the breakdown of organic remains.

Rubbish bin

Keep a small pot or old bucket close to the compost bin. When you dig out the compost, you will almost inevitably unearth old labels, plastic items, garden string and other non-perishable materials. Rather than add them to your garden soil, collect them for disposal.

Don't add soil

Do not deliberately add layers of soil to a compost heap. It was once thought that this was a necessary way of supplying bacteria but they are adequately plentiful on old plant remains and a layer of soil will merely block the free flow of air and water.

Mushroom compost: pros and cons

Mushroom compost can be a valuable organic soil amendment and mulching material. Before buying large quantities, however, you should be aware that it frequently contains significant amounts of limestone which would be beneficial on an acid soil but not on an alkaline one. Some mushroom composts have also been heavily dosed with insecticides which might taint vegetable crops so check with the suppliers if this is likely to be so.

Which compost?

The longer you plan to keep a plant in a container, the higher the number of John Innes potting compost you should choose: No. 3 will be necessary for very long-term plantings.

Peat alternative

For a reliable alternative to peat-based composts for many purposes, choose those based on coir dust (a waste product of the coconut industry).

Once-only compost

Never re-use old seedling compost – the nutrient will have been partly used up and disease organisms may be present.

Compost fork

For lifting compost or manure, a garden fork is not the ideal tool. If you do a good deal of muck shifting, it is worth searching for a second-hand farmer's manure fork, which has several more tines than a garden fork and a dipped central area to prevent the material from slipping off.

6

Watering, mulching and drainage

Legal hosing

Most water authorities require a non-return valve to be fitted on a tap to which a hose-pipe is attached. To be on the right side of the law, you too should have one. They can be bought relatively cheaply.

Each water authority has its own rules regarding the use of unattended hoses and sprinklers: some require you to purchase a licence. Do check before you embark on any garden watering.

Cover up your rainwater

Use a cover on a rainwater butt to minimize any contamination of the water with pest and disease organisms.

Tap water is fine

Even if you live in an area where the water is hard, you will be most unlikely to cause harm to any plants, even lime-hating species, by using it for watering, with the possible exception of rhododendrons and azaleas in pots.

Do-it-yourself drainage

If your garden is regularly very waterlogged, it may be worthwhile installing a drainage system. This can be done relatively inexpensively and without undertaking massive excavations by using one of the kits specially sold for garden use.

Instant bog

If you don't have the time, energy or inclination to drain a wet area of your garden, why not create a bog garden using wetland plants and having a pool at the centre?

Non-slip hosepipe

For ease of connecting a hosepipe, have an outside tap with a screw thread installed.

Clay for capillary matting

For the best results with capillary matting for watering plant pots, use clay not plastic pots, which generally have a slight indentation at the base preventing them from making good contact with the mat.

Regulate your flow

For the most efficient use of unattended garden watering equipment, always attach some form of automatic water-flow regulator to your tap. This will switch the water off (and some will even switch it on) after predetermined lengths of time have passed or volumes of water been delivered.

Choose the right sprinkler

Be sure to choose a sprinkler that most suits your garden needs. There are many modern types, varying not only in the area that they cover but also in the shape of the area over which the water is delivered. There is little point in having a sprinkler that waters your neighbour's garden as well as your own.

Watering by pot

In dry seasons, one way of ensuring that water reaches where it is needed is to sink plastic plant pots in the soil close to the thirsty plants. Fill these with water which will slowly seep out of the bottom rather than run off the surface or quickly evaporate.

Irrigation only

If you use a trickle irrigation system, either in the greenhouse or garden, never be tempted to apply liquid fertilizer through it – this will encourage algal growth which will block the nozzles.

Gentle watering

Use a purpose-made perforated hose laid on the ground to give the gentlest possible watering among herbaceous plants.

Seedlings

Leave cans of water overnight in the greenhouse to warm up before watering tender young seedlings as they can be damaged by the shock of cold water.

Use a children's watering can to provide the gentlest of watering for seed trays.

Don't overfill pots

When filling plant containers, leave the compost surface about 2–3 cm (1 in) below the rim to allow room for watering without washing out the contents.

Best time to water

Always water plants in the evening during hot weather so the water has a chance to soak round the roots before it is evaporated by the sun.

When to water most

Water garden plants most when the objects of their cultivation are maturing – flowers as the buds open, lettuces as they heart up, potatoes as the tubers start to form (at flowering time) and so forth.

Self-watering baskets

If you go away on holiday during hot weather, hanging baskets can usually be kept going by lifting them down from their brackets and standing them on buckets or bowls of water in a shady position. The plants emerging from directly underneath may suffer but the basket as a whole should survive.

African violets

Be careful not to wet the leaves when watering African violets as this causes them to rot. Stand the pot in water overnight so that water is taken up from below and then allow it to drain the next morning.

Conifer mulch on peat

Use pine needles or other conifer litter as a mulch on a peat bed or peat garden.

Use bark wisely

Chipped or shredded bark is an effective mulch, but because it is so expensive use it on beds close to the house where its attractive appearance will be put to best effect.

First rot your mowings

Do not use uncomposted lawn mowings or other green matter as a mulch: they will begin to rot *in situ* and temporarily deplete the soil of nitrogen as they do so.

Camellias

Be sure that camellias are well mulched in the autumn – they are very prone to drop their flower buds and the commonest reason for this is that the roots are beginning to dry out.

7

Tools and equipment

Stainless steel is best

For the ultimate in ease and pleasure of use, combined with simplicity of maintenance, choose stainless steel garden tools.

Interchangeable tools

To put together a set of garden tools at minimum cost, select a range with detachable heads. In this way, one handle can be used with hoes, rakes and other cultivation appliances.

Peaceful Sundays

Try to avoid using powered garden tools on Sundays, especially on Sunday afternoons, when they will disturb the neighbours.

Choose your weight

Never buy a garden tool of any type until you have had the chance to handle it. Weight and balance are very important criteria and can only be judged by each individual gardener.

Spick and span

Always wipe over your tools with an oily cloth before putting them away; it takes only a few moments but may add years to their lives.

Essential items

If you don't want, or can't afford, a complete set of garden tools, your priority purchases should be: a border fork, a border spade, a weeding fork, a trowel, a spring-tine rake and a Dutch or similar hoe.

Lead-free lawnmowers

Most modern lawnmowers and other petrol-engined garden equipment will run on lead-free petrol. Check first with the equipment manufacturers but use it if you can.

Chain saw warning

Think several times before buying and using a chain saw in the garden. They are extremely dangerous tools and should be used with the utmost care, according to the manufacturers' guidelines. Never use one without familiarizing yourself with the instructions, and under no circumstances when you are alone or standing on a ladder or branch.

Safe shear sharpening

Don't be tempted to try sharpening high quality secateurs or shears yourself – take them to an authorized service agent.

Choose the right tines

Use straight slasher rather than L-shaped tines on a rotary cultivator, especially on clayey soils, to avoid smearing and forming an impenetrable layer below the surface.

Care for your secateurs

After pruning, clean the resinous sap from secateurs, and disinfect them at the same time by wiping them thoroughly with a cloth soaked in meths.

Which wheelbarrow?

If you have large areas of fairly soft ground in your garden or have to push your wheelbarrow across the lawn fairly frequently, why not choose one with a ball-pattern wheel? These are remarkably easy to push, won't compact the ground and can even be fitted with an extension top to enable bulky grass mowings to be carried easily.

Compatible hoses

When buying hose accessories, it makes sense to stick to the products of one of the major manufacturers for you may find that not all equipment is compatible and you could end up with annoying leaks.

Spotless pots

Always clean pots and seed trays carefully before re-using them. First wash off any soil or compost, then dip them in a proprietary garden disinfectant before finally rinsing them in clean water and allowing them to dry in the open air.

8

Health and safety

Anchor your ladder

When working from a ladder in the garden, always use a short length of rope to lash it to a branch or other support.

Walk the plank

When planting or doing other work in a garden pool, don't be tempted to lean out too far – it is much safer and easier to lay large planks or even a ladder across and work from them. But never allow children to try this.

Goggles in the garden

Always wear goggles when using garden shredders, chain saws, strimmers or hedge trimmers.

Splinters

To remove a splinter from your finger, put a little damp sugar over the affected area and then apply a piece of sticking plaster. After two or three days the skin will have softened and the splinter will be forced to the surface.

Bonemeal

Wear lightweight rubber gloves when handling bonemeal. Although it is most unlikely to carry any harmful diseases, it is wise to be on the safe side, especially if you have cuts on your hands.

Avoid farm chemicals

Only use chemicals specifically sold for use in gardens. The use of farm chemicals is not only illegal but also potentially dangerous as they may be of higher concentration and require special handling and application procedures.

Keep chemicals wrapped

Never store garden chemicals in anything other than their original packaging; and always keep them out of reach of children.

Pet-proof fertilizer

If you are concerned about the possibility of pets picking up lawn fertilizer or weedkiller on their feet, always use a liquid formulation.

Noxious fumes

Where gardens adjoin busy main roads there is a risk of lead from petrol fumes contaminating vegetable crops. This can be minimized by not growing vegetables within about 7 m (25 ft) of the road and by planting a fairly thick barrier hedge such as hawthorn.

Make sure of your mushrooms

Don't eat any mushrooms or toadstools found on your lawn or elsewhere without having your identification checked by someone knowledgeable.

Laburnum

Although there is dispute among the medical fraternity on the actual harm occasioned to children through eating laburnum, this, together with yew, is a plant probably best not planted in a garden where there are very young children.

Dangerous cacti

Be extremely careful when handling cacti: even those with few obvious spines, like the species of *Mammillaria*, may have myriads of minute prickles concealed within a 'woolly' mass and these can be very painful and difficult to remove from the skin.

Irritant sap

Many plants have irritant sap. Among common house and conservatory plants, those that should be handled especially carefully for this reason are poinsettias, dieffenbachias and oleanders.

Irritating caterpillars

Never pick up the very hairy 'woolly bear' types of caterpillar often found in gardens for the hairs can irritate.

9

Pests and diseases

Look below the leaf

When checking plants for the presence of caterpillars and other pests, remember that they are more likely to be beneath the leaves than on top.

Encourage birds

Have a bird table and boxes to attract birds to your garden. The problems that birds cause to fruit and other garden plants are more than offset by the good they do in helping to keep down pests.

Pirimicarb for aphids

To avoid harming beneficial insects in the garden, use the insecticide pirimicarb to control aphids. It is selective for this group of insects.

Bats against pests

Erect a bat roosting box in your garden – not only to conserve the bats but also because they will help keep garden pests in check. A bat box is similar to a bird box but with a larger opening – your local natural history society will advise on its construction.

Hazards of honeytraps

Never put out honey in wasp traps or for other purposes. It will attract bees which may pick up disease from it or, at best, be encouraged to steal honey from other hives.

Red spider mites

Mist house and greenhouse plants frequently to minimize the problem of red spider mites.

Rabbits

To keep out rabbits, fencing must be buried at least 30 cm (1 ft) in the soil.

Woodlice

The best way to control woodlice is by finding and clearing away their hiding places – under logs, pots or piles of old seed trays, for instance.

Cats

In a walled or fenced garden, you can deter cats by fixing a single or paired strand of wire about 8 cm (3 in) above the top of the boundary – this prevents the cats from being able to balance.

Moles

Moles are most likely to be controlled by the insertion of traps into their runs but the positioning of the traps is best done by someone experienced. In rural areas, farmers will generally know of a local person skilled in mole trapping.

Beneficial mites

The large red mites often found crawling round the garden are not red spider mites and should not be destroyed – they are actually beneficial because they prey on other harmful species. The real red spider mites are barely visible to the naked eye, and are not in fact noticeably red.

Safe disposal

Dispose of unwanted pesticides by washing them with copious amounts of water down an outside foul drain (one connected to a sewerage system).

Mealy bugs

You can fairly effectively control limited attacks by mealy bugs on cacti and other plants by touching each colony with a paint brush dipped in methylated spirit.

Earwigs

Trap earwigs among dahlias, chrysanthemums and other plants by filling plastic plant pots with straw or hay and supporting them, upturned, on the ends of bamboo canes. The earwigs will hide in the pots during the daytime when they can be removed and destroyed.

Ancient history

When holes appear mysteriously on the leaves of garden plants, look closely at their margins. If they are brown, this indicates that the damage occurred some time ago and it is pointless looking for the culprits.

Caterpillars

If caterpillar attacks on brassicas become too extensive to control by hand-picking, and if you are not enthusiastic about using chemical sprays, try the biological control method of spraying with a culture of the bacterium *Bacillus thuringiensis*. This is harmless to everything except caterpillars and can be purchased from garden centres.

Slugs

Grow hostas in pots or other containers if slugs are a problem on plants growing in the open ground.

Narcissus fly

After the stems and foliage have been cut down on daffodil bulbs, rake some soil into the hole left above the bulb to deter the egg-laying activities of the narcissus fly.

Whitefly or aphids?

If you use a biological control system to combat whitefly or red spider mite in a greenhouse, you will be unable to use insecticides against aphids or other pests.

Cabbage root flies

To control cabbage root fly, cut 10–12 cm (4–5 in) diameter discs of felt carpet underlay. Cut a hole approximately 2 cm (1 in) in diameter in the centre of each and then make a radial cut to enable the disc to be slotted round the base of each plant. Ensure that it lies flat on the soil and this will dissuade the female fly from laying her eggs.

Slugs

Use ash from the fire grate or some fine spiny twigs such as gorse around lettuce and other plants to deter slugs.

Carrot flies

Use a 60 cm (2 ft) high fence of plastic sheet around beds of carrots to deter low-flying female carrot flies from entering the crop to lay their eggs.

Spiders

If you find a spider in your house, don't kill it or throw it out, transfer it to the greenhouse where it will set up home and help to catch pests.

Mice and voles

If mice and voles are a serious problem among newly sown pea crops or elsewhere in the garden, it may be necessary to place traps among the plants; but never leave a mouse trap in the open – always be sure that some netting is placed over the top to ensure that birds are not caught by it.

Pea moth

If pea moth is troublesome, try sowing some seeds earlier and some later than usual in order to avoid having many plants in flower during June and July when the female moths are laying their eggs.

Colorado beetle

Keep an eye open for the black-and-buff-striped, ladybird-like Colorado beetles on potatoes and related plants. This is an alien pest, not established in Britain. Any insects found should be trapped in a box and the nearest police station or office of the Ministry of Agriculture notified.

Soot

Soot is of some value as a fertilizer but perhaps its best use in the garden is when it is scattered in the planting holes with seed potato tubers where it appears to have the effect of deterring slugs.

Leatherjackets

Leatherjackets are not easy to control in the vegetable garden, but very thorough cultivation of soil will bring them to the surface where they will fall prey to the local bird population.

Fruit trees

Even if you feel that pest control in general is not worthwhile on fruit trees, a tar oil spray in winter on young trees and on soft fruit canes and bushes makes sound sense: it will kill overwintering pests but must only be applied while the tree is dormant.

Codling moth

Don't waste time tying sacking or similar material round apple trees to trap the codling moth. It will have no impact on the amount of damage to be expected in the following year for insects will fly in from neighbouring trees.

Winter moths

When applying protection to fruit trees against winter moth attack, use specially formulated grease in bands on the trunk. Car or other type of grease is not suitable, and the sticky paper bands sold for the purpose will not adhere closely enough to rough bark to prevent the insects from crawling underneath.

Propiconazole

The fungicide propiconazole is ideal for controlling rust disease on roses, antirrhinums and other ornamentals but must not be used on edible crops; there you must rely on fungicides, such as Bordeaux mixture, that contain copper.

Damping off disease

If you find damping off disease in a seed tray, dispose of the entire contents: even apparently healthy seedlings will almost certainly have fungal growth on their roots and result in feeble plants. Disinfect the tray before re-use.

Clubroot

Always raise your own brassica and wallflower seedlings to avoid the possibility of bringing clubroot into your garden on transplant roots.

To protect brassica plants from clubroot, raise each plant in an individual pot of about 12 cm (5 in) diameter and plant out in the entire pot ball of compost.

Diseased wallflowers

If you find dark-coloured wallflowers with yellowish stripes on the petals, destroy the plants promptly – they are contaminated with a virus that can spread to brassicas.

Pansy sickness

If you have trouble in persuading pansies or violas to establish in your garden, the problem may be pansy sickness in the soil. To overcome this, raise each plant in a small individual pot of compost and plant it out in this, complete with the compost ball.

Potato blight

If blight attacks occur on maincrop potatoes, cut off the haulm of the plants and destroy it (not by composting). Then wait at least two weeks before lifting the tubers for storage in order to give spores in the soil time to die out.

Potato scab

Where scab is a problem on potatoes, never apply lime to the soil, and keep the potatoes well watered as they come into flower. Try digging in green lawn mowings to the plot at the rate of about three bucketfuls per square metre (yard).

Parsnip canker

Where parsnip canker disease is a problem, choose the variety 'Avonresister'.

Honey fungus

The spread of honey fungus from a diseased tree stump can be minimized by burying heavy duty plastic sheets vertically in the soil to a depth of at least 60 cm (2 ft) to isolate the tree from others nearby. The position of the slit trench should preferably be beyond the limits of the tree's root system.

Mildew

In spring, keep an eye open for the first signs of mildew on the shoot tips of apple trees and nip off the affected parts. It is from these initial disease spots that mildew spreads and, on young trees, it is possible to contain the problem effectively by this simple expedient.

Brown rot fungus

Knock off any diseased and shrivelled apples still hanging on the trees during the winter: they will almost certainly be harbouring the brown rot fungus which would affect the next year's crop.

Silver leaf disease

If a plum tree develops the symptoms of silver leaf disease, wait for at least a season to see if it recovers – they often do. If silvering appears on any suckers, however, this is an indication that the disease fungus is established in the rootstock and the tree should then be grubbed up and burned.

Big bud

If you see the symptoms of big bud on blackcurrant bushes, this is an indication that they are contaminated with virus and should be replaced.

10

Weeds and weed control, and chemicals

Weedkiller caution

Read the instructions on weedkiller packets at least twice to be sure that you have the correct product for each task.

Soil indicators

The types of weeds growing in your garden (or nearby) can give useful information about your soil.

Damp soil: rushes, horsetail, knot-grass, lady's smock, ragged robin.

Alkaline soil: burnet, stemless thistle, bladder campion, wild thyme.

Poor soil: quaking grass, Yorkshire fog, sheep's sorrel, spurrey, ragwort.

Acid or lime deficient soil: bracken, spurrey, sheep's sorrel, field bindweed, oxeye daisy, mayweed.

Good or loamy soil: buttercup, coltsfoot, stinging nettle, groundsel, goosefoot, cleavers, dandelion, chick weed, sow thistle.

Heavy soil: coltsfoot, couch, horsetail, creeping buttercup, dandelion, dock.

Safe storage

Never store garden chemicals in the open. Large bags or sacks are best placed on some form of rack or other support that will allow air to circulate beneath.

Broadcast by birds

Make a point of regularly pulling out seedlings that arise from seeds dropped beneath bird tables: it is always possible that a significant weed species could become established in your garden if they are allowed to grow unchecked.

Rules for spraying

Never spray any garden chemical in windy or frosty weather.

When using a garden sprayer, adjust the nozzle to give the finest mist that settles fairly rapidly without being blown away by the wind.

Any watering cans or sprayers that have been used for weedkiller should be clearly marked and not used for watering or for applying any other garden chemical.

Never apply weedkiller or pesticide through a hose-end diluter.

Contact-acting insecticides and fungicides must be sprayed more carefully than systemic types (the small print on the packet will tell you which you have). This is because contact sprays only work if they make contact with the organism; systemic types are taken up into the sap and spread throughout the plant.

Keep allotments tidy

If you have an allotment, always keep it weed- and rubbish-free – you owe it to your fellow allotment holders, quite apart from any requirements that may be written into your agreement.

Separate chemicals

Never mix together two different types of garden chemical (an insecticide and fungicide, for instance) unless the manufacturers state specifically that this may be done.

Don't cultivate your couch

Never use a rotary cultivator on land infested with couch grass: it will very effectively chop up the rhizomes and distribute them even further through the soil.

Hoe and mulch

The two most useful ways of controlling annual weeds are by using a Dutch or similar pattern push hoe and plenty of organic mulch, in a layer at least 5 cm (2 in) thick.

Groundsel warning

When using a Dutch hoe for weeding, bear in mind that while most weeds will shrivel once chopped through, a few (groundsel most notably) will continue to flower and set seed and so should be raked up and disposed of.

Keep tabs on your weedkiller

When applying weedkiller among growing plants from a watering can fitted with a trickle bar, be sure to tape on the trickler firmly. If it drops off, you could cause serious damage to your precious vegetation.

Glyphosate

Check the weather forecast carefully before taking the time, trouble and expense of using a weedkiller containing glyphosate – six hours of dryness must elapse after application in order for the chemical to be taken up effectively; and the hotter the weather, the more effective will it be.

Weedkiller shield

When using the weedkiller glyphosate, cut a 20 cm (8 in) long piece of c. 2 cm (1 in) diameter plastic pipe and use this as a shield by spraying down it when treating weeds among valuable plants.

Sodium chlorate

The weedkiller sodium chlorate should be used only on sites well away from plants. It is not only a persistent and total weedkiller but it will also creep some distance through the soil.

Blue lawns

Use a grass collector on your mower to minimize the spread of the blue-flowered creeping speedwell on lawns. This plant does not set seed in Britain but mowing without a collector provides an ideal method for the production and dispersal of its cuttings.

Weedkiller contamination

After a lawn has been treated with weedkiller, don't use compost made from the mowings for at least six months.

Bindweed

Where bindweed is entangled with a hedge or other shrubby plant and can't readily be sprayed with weed-killer, carefully untwine a few of the shoots, damaging them as little as possible, then lay them on the ground and spray them with weedkiller containing glyphosate.

If you are really persistent, you may be able to keep on top of a bindweed infestation by repeatedly hoeing off the shoot tips as they emerge. Old gardeners who hoed in this way at the end of every week called it the 'never let them see a Monday' method.

Horsetail

It may be possible to eradicate the deep-rooted weed horsetail in areas such as allotments, where no peren-nial plants complicate the matter, by laying black poly-thene sheets over the soil surface for at least one, preferably two, seasons.

Couch grass

Do not compost the rhizomes of couch grass for if the composting process does not completely destroy them you will spread the problem further around your garden. Rhizomes should be dried and burned or bagged up and taken to the local tip.

In order to eradicate couch grass from among other plants, use the weedkiller alloxydim-sodium which is specific for couch and a small number of other perennial grasses.

The total weedkillers paraquat and glyphosate both act, although in different ways, through green tissue. They may safely be used among established shrubs therefore, as any chemical that splashes on to the bark of mature stems causes no harm.

Trojan horses

When buying new plants in containers, always scrape away the top few centimetres of compost and dispose of it before the new specimen is placed in your garden. Soil-less composts especially tend to harbour seeds and seedlings of the hairy bitter-cress, a most troublesome annual weed.

Dandelions

You must take especial care when digging out dandelions for they can regenerate from any part of the taproot. Other deep-rooted weeds such as docks can generally only do so from the top 10 cm (4 in) or so.

11

Propagation

Top up with sand

When striking cuttings in seed trays, half fill the tray
with potting compost then top it up with a layer of sand.
Push in the cuttings so that their base just penetrates the
compost layer.

Root cuttings

When taking root cuttings, make a sloping cut at the top
of each root length and a straight cut at the bottom;
otherwise you will not be able to tell the difference and
may well insert them upside-down into the compost.

Rooting powder

When using hormone rooting powder, be sure to knock
off any excess powder – at high concentrations, rooting
powder can inhibit rather than encourage root growth.

Always use hormone rooting powder when taking
softwood cuttings; in addition to the actual rooting
stimulation, the powder contains fungicide which will
lessen the chances of rotting.

Renew your rooting powder every season; and be
sure to keep it dry.

Leafy cuttings

When potting up cuttings that have leafy stems, be sure to pull or cut away the lower leaves so there is no contact between leaves and compost, which tends to result in rotting.

Remember that the secret of success with leafy cuttings is preventing moisture loss through the leaves; a good cover on the propagator to maintain a moist environment is essential.

Transplanting

Try to transplant on dull days when the water loss through the leaves will be lower and the plants are given less of a shock by the move.

Don't bother cutting off some of the leaves of transplants to minimize water loss – it has little beneficial effect. Ensuring that the surrounding soil is saturated is of much more use.

Cold frame

Always place a cold frame used for hardening off seedlings in at least partial shade not full sun where the young plants will inevitably dry out quickly and may be scorched.

A frame used for rooting cuttings should always be placed in the shade in order to keep the cuttings cool and moist.

Heather

To multiply your stock of heather plants, pile a mound of soil in the centre of a large clump: the old shoots will root in this, giving you masses of small layers that can be cut off and replanted.

Herbaceous perennials

Be careful when weeding under herbaceous perennials – there may well be self-sown seedlings that you can pot up and use elsewhere.

Small plants

If plants that you have raised from seed or purchased from a garden centre are on the small side, keep them in their pots for a season, and regularly give them liquid fertilizer in order to build them up before planting in the garden.

Succulents

When separating offsets (shoots with roots attached) from succulents and other plants for potting on, use a sharp knife to sever the connecting stem but then leave the offset undisturbed for a few weeks to develop good roots before moving it.

Cacti

When taking cuttings from cacti, allow the cut surface to dry for a few hours before potting up – this will allow sufficient healing to take place to lessen the likelihood of decay setting in.

Mistletoe

Induce mistletoe to grow on old apple trees by inserting a ripe seed (taken from a mistletoe growing on another old apple) into a slit on the underside of a branch. Seal the slit with clay.

Holly

Don't be surprised if you have difficulty in striking cuttings of trees or shrubs, like holly, that have very closely grained wood or tissues that exude quantities of gummy latex: they are notoriously tricky to deal with.

Globe artichokes

Propagate globe artichokes by taking offsets in April and planting them directly into their permanent positions.

Camellias

Camellias can be difficult to strike from stem cuttings so try leaf bud cuttings instead. Cut 2 cm (1 in) lengths of stem, each bearing a single leaf and its associated bud, and push them into the surface of the compost with the leaf uppermost.

Fuchsias

Early in the year, take shoot tip cuttings of fuchsias that have been overwintered in the greenhouse. They will strike very readily and give you plenty of small plants for use in bedding and containers.

Lily bulbs

Multiply lily bulbs by pulling away three or four (but preferably no more) of the overlapping scales. Put them in a plastic bag in damp peat or vermiculite and keep them in the airing cupboard for about six weeks, by which time roots should have formed and each can be potted up. Plants grown from these scales should reach flowering size in about three years.

Primroses

Divide cultivated varieties of primroses and other primulas every two or three years to maintain their vitality.

Layering

For a reliable way of propagating difficult shrubs, especially evergreens, try layering them. Make a nick on the underside of a low-hanging branch and peg it firmly into the soil. Roots should form within twelve or eighteen months, when the branch can be severed from its parent.

12

Seed sowing

Keeping seed

If you are keeping seed from your own plants, only do so from ones that are perfectly healthy and show no signs of disease, and don't bother to save seed from F_1 hybrid varieties (see information on seed packet) which will not come true.

Sterilizing compost

Use a microwave oven to sterilize seedling or other compost – treat 1 kg (2 lb) at a time at full setting for three minutes in a non-metallic dish.

Long-life seeds

To make seeds last longer, store them in their packets in glass screw-top jars in the fridge, with a small sachet of silica gel drying agent in each jar.

Is it too wet?

If the soil sticks to your boots when you walk over it, it is too wet for sowing seeds.

Sowing depth

A good rule of thumb when sowing seeds in pots or seed trays is to cover them with a depth of compost equivalent to twice their own diameter.

Simple seed drill

The simplest way to prepare an accurate seed drill is by pressing gently into the soil with the back of a garden rake. Simpler still, but slightly less satisfactory because it doesn't firm the soil, is to drag a bamboo cane along the surface.

Water before sowing

In order to aid seedling emergence, water seed drills lightly *before* the seed is sown, not after. In this way, there is no danger of forming a barrier to growth in the shape of a crust or cap on the soil surface.

Mixed seedlings

When pricking on seedlings grown from packets of mixed varieties, use some of the smaller as well as the more robust seedlings to be sure of obtaining the full range of varieties and colour.

Saving seeds

When saving seeds from your own plants, place bags over the dying flower heads to catch the seeds as they fall – but always use cellophane, not plastic bags, which do not 'breathe', so causing mould to develop within.

Free-flowing seed

To distribute seeds uniformly from a packet, crease it at 90° to its fold and tap the seeds out from this new crease – if you use the original fold, the bend is so acute that seeds become trapped in it and do not flow out easily.

Surface sowing

Very tiny seeds, such as those of lobelia, have too small a food reserve for the seedling to grow any distance before it requires light, so such seeds should always be scattered on the surface and not buried.

Fluid-sowing kit

If you have difficulty in obtaining good germination and emergence with celery, parsley or other 'difficult' seeds, buy a fluid-sowing kit; this provides a means of pre-germinating the seeds and so ensures a uniform crop.

Tiny seeds

Mix a little finely ground brick dust with tiny seeds such as those of fibrous-rooted begonias in order to help you to sow them thinly and also enable you to see where you have sown.

Exotic plants

If you have difficulty in germinating hard-seeded exotic plants, especially Australian species, try placing the seeds on the surface of sand in a clay pot, lay some hay or straw on the top and set fire to it. Then incubate the seeds in the usual way.

Fibrous-rooted begonias

Seed of fibrous-rooted begonias can be difficult to germinate; sow it on the surface of the compost and maintain a temperature of 21°C.

Cyclamen

Soak cyclamen seeds in warm (40°C) water for 24 hours before sowing and then keep the seed trays in the dark until the seeds have germinated.

Vegetables

It is pointless keeping large seeds such as peas and beans for more than one season because their germination will decline markedly. Most smaller vegetable seeds should keep well, however, under careful storage for at least two seasons, and brassicas especially will remain viable for several years.

Tiny seedlings

Always prick out tiny seedlings such as lobelias in small clumps rather than trying to separate individual plants.

Mustard and cress

When sowing mustard and cress seeds, sow the slower germinating cress three days before adding the mustard.

Tomatoes

Allow nine weeks between sowing tomato seeds and the time you intend to plant them.

Sweet peas

Nick dark-seeded sweet peas on the side of the seed opposite the eye in order to aid germination.

Primulas

Always sow primula seeds on the surface of the compost and do not allow the temperature to rise above 21°C. Be prepared even so for prolonged and irregular germination.

Moisten before sowing

Instead of soaking sweet pea, pea and runner bean seeds in water before planting, wrap them overnight in damp tissue paper. This gives more consistent results.

Pea seeds

The round seeded varieties of pea are hardier than the wrinkled seeded types. Always use round seeded peas for autumn sowing therefore.

13

Pruning

Pruning tools

If you have a great deal of pruning to do, it is worth buying a curved pruning saw which will enable you to work between closely placed branches. In extreme conditions, where branches are very crowded, use a wire saw.

Despite what the older gardening books may tell you, a pruning knife is not a tool for the inexperienced; secateurs are much safer.

When pruning, never twist secateurs. If it is impossible to cut through a branch with straight, downward pressure, then you need a more powerful tool such as a pair of loppers.

For the gentlest pruning action, use bypass or scissor-action secateurs: they will be least likely to damage soft stems. But use single-bladed anvil secateurs to cut hard woody tissues most effectively.

First principles

Always make pruning cuts to about 0.5 cm (¼ in) above a bud, sloping away from the bud itself in order not to leave a stub where diseases could establish.

When pruning any plant, the first task should be to cut out any obviously dead or diseased shoots.

If you remember that one of the main objectives of pruning is to allow light and air to penetrate to the centre of the plant, you will not go far wrong.

Flowering shrubs

Flowering shrubs and climbers that flower before midsummer should be pruned in the autumn. Those that flower after midsummer should be pruned in the spring.

Trees

When cutting off branches from trees, do not cut into the small swollen collar at the branch base or the wound will not heal satisfactorily.

After cutting branches off trees, do not paint the cut surface with bitumen or other wound-sealing compound: it will be of no benefit and may actually cause harm by sealing in fungal spores and hindering the healing process.

If you are in any doubt about when and how to prune a tree or shrub, do nothing at all. The plant will not suffer and you will not ruin its shape or flowering which can happen if you prune wrongly.

Suckers

Pull away, rather than cut, suckers that appear at the base of roses, rhododendrons and other shrubs. By cutting them, you will simply encourage more suckers to arise.

Eucalyptus

Prune eucalyptus shoots hard back in early spring to stimulate the production of young shoots bearing the rounded foliage which is so useful for flower arranging.

Pampas grass

Never clear out old growth on pampas grass by setting fire to it: use a stout pair of gloves and pull it out by hand.

Shape your shrubs

When pruning, you can dictate the shape of a shrub or tree by carefully selecting the buds above which you make your pruning cut. Choose outward-facing buds to give a spreading, open appearance and inward-facing ones for a more upright habit. The latter is often useful with such plants as plums where the weight of the fruit crop may break wide-spreading and brittle branches.

Root pruning

It is sometimes possible to restrain a vigorous tree by root pruning but this should never be done with those species, like plums, that are very prone to form suckers. Cut a trench 45 cm (18 in) deep and position it at a distance from the trunk calculated by allowing about 30 cm (1 ft) for every 2.5 cm (1 in) of trunk diameter. Sever the thickest roots but leave the finer ones and then refill the hole.

Prune for more colour

To obtain the best shoot colour on the shrubby ornamental dogwoods like *Cornus alba* 'Sibirica', prune them back hard to about 30–45 cm (12–18 in) above soil level in spring.

Chop up for compost

If you don't have a garden shredder, chop up prunings into small pieces with your secateurs before putting them on the compost heap.

Frosty pruning

It is a myth that apple trees shouldn't be pruned in frosty weather. I have done this on many occasions and it provides warming and useful exercise at a time when there is often little else that can be done in the garden.

Deciduous trees

Although little harm will generally be caused if deciduous trees are pruned when in full leaf, remember that the considerable bulk that the leaves themselves add will make for extra work in disposing of the branches.

Smooth trunks

To give the smoothest, most attractive trunk on those trees such as birches that are grown for the beauty of their bark, rub out promptly any leaves or shoots that may arise on the main stem. If you leave them until they develop into small branches and require proper pruning, unappealing scars will result.

Shrubs against walls

Foliage shrubs trained against walls should be pruned or clipped in winter if deciduous, or in early spring if evergreen.

When pruning any plant trained against a wall, your first course of action should be to remove any branches growing directly away from or directly towards the wall itself.

Fruit trees

When following instructions for pruning fruit trees, you need to know the difference between fruit buds and leaf buds: the former are plump and the latter long and thin.

An unpruned fruit tree will begin cropping earlier than one that is pruned, but if left unpruned, the tree will soon have a mass of tangled branches bearing fewer and smaller fruit.

Prune by degrees

When pruning a severely neglected tree, especially a fruit tree, don't undertake all of the work at once. Spread the job over three seasons to cause the least shock to the plant.

Cordon fruit trees

When summer-pruning cordon fruit trees, work on the pears before the apples as their wood hardens earlier in the season.

Bud nicking

Shoot growth from dormant buds can be influenced by bud nicking. A small nick made in the bark just above a bud will help stimulate growth; one made below it tends to weaken it.

Companion pruning

Remember that if you grow two plants very closely together – allowing a climber to grow through a shrub, for instance – the effect may well look attractive but be sure that you are still able to prune each of them satisfactorily and at the appropriate times.

Plums

Plums and damsons should not be pruned in late autumn and winter as other fruit trees are because this will expose the tissues to infection by the silver leaf fungus. Prune them instead in late spring or early summer.

Large branches

When removing a large branch from a tree, first cut a wedge-shaped piece from the underside before sawing through from above. This will prevent the weight of the branch tearing tissue away from the main trunk of the tree as it falls.

14

Hedges and fences

Growth regulators

Use chemical hedge-growth regulators only on the types of plant specifically suggested by the manufacturers. They are, for instance, not suitable for yew or box.

Extra food and water required

Remember that the soil at the base of a fence, hedge or wall is abnormally dry and so plants in such positions will need extra watering; at the foot of a hedge, the soil will also be impoverished and in need of additional fertilizer.

Box

Never cut back box bushes or hedges very hard into the old wood: unlike yew, they will not regenerate as satisfactorily.

Level hedge

When cutting along the top of a hedge, unless you have a very good eye for a straight line, erect a taut string, tied to two stakes and levelled with a spirit level.

When to cut

Unless the weather is very mild, don't cut hedges before April or after October.

Birds' nests

When cutting hedges for the first time in the spring, do try and be sure there are no nesting birds that will be disturbed.

Laurel

When cutting laurel hedges, a pair of secateurs is the ideal tool because the large leaves look unsightly and may turn brown if sliced through with shears. Sadly, many laurel hedges are too large to make this practical.

An ornamental hedge

When planting a hedge that doesn't need to be too tough or robust, why not consider using ornamental flowering shrubs? Such types as berberis, *Rosa rugosa*, cotoneasters, forsythia and flowering currant can look most attractive.

Lavender

For the best variety of lavender for hedging choose 'Hidcote'.

Topiary

The best shrub to use for topiary is yew, followed by box and holly.

If you want to decorate your garden with topiary,

remember that while individual shrubs can fairly easily be trimmed attractively, it is extremely difficult to trim accurately a *matching* pair.

The more fanciful topiary shapes can only be formed over a firm metal framework and you will become extremely annoyed and frustrated with your efforts if this is not in place before planting.

The toughest hedge

The most durable, tough and stock-proof hedging plant is undoubtedly hawthorn, which has stood the test of time as a farmland boundary.

Another of the toughest, densest and yet most unappreciated hedging plants is *Tsuga heterophylla*. With only one cut each year, it will form an almost impenetrable and yet very attractive boundary.

Hedges need mulch

Don't forget your hedges when watering and mulching. The benefits to a hedge of an annual mulch of manure or compost are very great in terms of the subsequent thickening of growth.

Instant barrier

If you require instant protection and privacy and yet really would prefer a hedge, why not erect a fence and then plant a hedge alongside, ultimately removing the fence when the hedge has reached the required height? But do remember to plant the hedge on the sunnier side of the fence.

Animal-proof

A way of making a hedge animal-proof, even when it is first planted, is to erect a heavy duty plastic wire fence (preferably of black or green plastic) and then place the hedging plants in a double row on either side. The netting will give protection, yet as the hedge grows, it will disappear within it and, being in the centre, not impede the trimming.

Holly

If the idea of a holly hedge appeals to you, remember that you will be unlikely to combine a neat appearance with berries because the trimming process will inevitably remove the flowers.

Long-life fence posts

When sinking wooden fence or other posts in the soil, wrap the base in a plastic bag which will lessen the rapidity of rotting and prolong its effective life.

Sink wooden fence posts at least 45 cm (18 in) deep for added strength and brace every alternate post with a diagonal.

Always place a small cap on the top of wooden fence posts to prevent rainwater from penetrating down the grain.

Fence preservative

Wooden fences require treating with preservative every few years. The best preservative is probably creosote but remember that it will cause harm to plants trained against the fence unless they are pulled well away first and no chemical is splashed on them. Deciduous plants will be least harmed when they are leafless in winter.

Deer

To keep out deer, you will need a strong, chain-link wire fence at least 2 m (6 ft) high.

Most efficient fence

The best type of fence for lessening the impact of the wind and giving shelter without itself being seriously damaged is one that is 50 per cent permeable – in other words, has equal areas of gaps and solid structure.

A barrier such as a fence, wall or hedge, will lessen the impact of the wind on the leeward side for a distance equal approximately to 10 times its height.

Walls and the law

In general, you may erect a wall without planning permission if it does not exceed 1 m (3 ft) in height when abutting on a highway used by vehicular traffic and in other cases does not exceed 2 m (6 ft) in height. You should always seek verification, however, as special rules may apply in certain areas or with listed buildings.

New hedges for old

Remember that old, traditionally planted hedges containing species such as hawthorn can very often be rejuvenated by being laid. This ancient technique comprises partially cutting through the shoots, bending them down at an angle and so stimulating the production of new growth. Even if you feel unable to tackle this yourself, there will usually be farm workers in rural areas capable of taking on the task.

15

Paths and paving

Natural walkways

In a new garden, don't lay down paths before you have thought about the way that the garden functions – and watch the directions in which people walk naturally to pass from one place to another. In general, these are where your paths should be positioned.

Timber!

While timber lengths can be very useful for edging a path, a path surface made entirely from timber can become dangerously slippery when wet.

Chipped bark

Use chipped bark to create an attractive garden pathway. It will need topping up annually with about half the initial volume of bark.

Fencing rail edging

Use half-round farm fencing rails anchored with pairs of hardwood pegs as path edging to contain chipped bark, gravel or other loose material.

Plastic paths

For neat and relatively mud-free pathways between vegetable beds, use 30 cm (1 ft) wide strips of heavy duty plastic netting, held in place with metal skewer-pattern tent pegs.

Gravel problem

Don't use gravel as a path surface close to areas such as the vegetable plot, where the soil will be dug regularly: muddy boots are notorious for carrying gravel paths with them.

Liven up your concrete

To create a more attractive appearance from an area paved with concrete slabs without incurring the cost of complete re-laying, lift a few randomly distributed slabs and replace them with bricks, cobbles or some other material. This will give a contrast in texture and break up the monotony.

Quick crazy paving

To achieve a quick crazy paving effect, lay rectangular concrete slabs and then smash them with a hammer.

Granite replicas

Original granite or similar setts are very expensive and difficult to obtain but there are now concrete replicas that very closely resemble the real thing – and, being of uniform thickness, are much easier to lay.

As wide as a wheelbarrow

When laying paths and installing gateways within the garden, do be sure that they are wide enough for wheelbarrows, lawnmowers and other equipment to pass along them.

Local looks best

When choosing gravel or chippings for a path or driveway, those derived from a local stone will generally look the most attractive and be the cheapest.

Heavy traffic

Bear in mind that the manner of laying slabs, setts or other paving material will need to be different if the area is to carry vehicular traffic rather than be merely for pedestrian use.

Watch your fingers and toes

Always use heavy duty gloves and strong boots when handling paving slabs: they are very heavy and will cause a great deal of harm if you trap your fingers or drop one on your foot.

Drainage

When laying a solid path such as one of concrete or close-fitting mortared slabs, slope it from the centre outwards to allow for drainage and, if water does still collect in a corner or other area, use a heavy duty masonry drill to make one or two drainage holes.

Grass = mud

Grass paths may look very attractive in summer, but remember that even with very little use in winter, they will soon become converted into mud pools.

Rake your gravel

Gravel or chipped stone paths should ideally be raked about once a fortnight to maintain the most attractive appearance.

Bricks

Don't use ordinary household bricks to make paths: they will very soon crumble with the effects of frost. Engineering bricks or purpose-made setts should be used instead.

Plants in your path

The monotony of a very wide path or driveway can be lessened by allowing creeping plants to grow in the cracks between slabs, or, in the case of gravel, directly through the surface at the edges.

16

The greenhouse, cloches and cold frames

Bigger is better

When choosing a greenhouse, work out the size that you think you need, and then buy one at least half as big again.

If you are short of space, why not consider a lean-to greenhouse which can often benefit from the heat of the adjoining house wall?

The right greenhouse for your house

Choose a greenhouse for its appearance as well as its function – an aluminium structure may look appropriate with a new house but seldom does with a traditionally built old one.

Hardwood is better

Choose durable red cedar rather than softwood for a wooden greenhouse unless you are prepared to paint it annually. Even cedar requires treating with a colourless preservative every two or three years.

Automatic ventilation

If you are out in the daytime or away from home a great deal, fit automatic vent openers to the greenhouse to prevent it from overheating.

Constant breeze

To obtain the benefit of constant air movement within the greenhouse, choose a heater with a low consumption motor on which the fan operates constantly while the heating elements cut in and out under thermostatic control.

Use a thermometer

Use a maximum and minimum thermometer in the greenhouse to be sure that your heater is working correctly and efficiently.

Ring culture for success

Use gravel ring culture beds for the easiest and most reliable method of growing tomatoes in a greenhouse.

Greenhouse grapevine

Plant a greenhouse grapevine just outside the greenhouse itself in the border soil and pass the leading shoot through a hole made in the base of the side wall.

Try using a grapevine to provide shading in a greenhouse – but be prepared for the chore of collecting up the leaves in autumn.

Early in the new year, untie horizontal rods of greenhouse vines and temporarily re-tie them slightly below the horizontal. This will encourage a more uniform breaking of the buds.

Keep rainwater out

Don't use water from an outside rainwater butt on plants in the greenhouse: it may well contain micro-organisms that, while harmless outdoors, could cause damage to young plants in warm conditions.

Safety first

If you plan to have mains electricity in your greenhouse, be sure to have the job done by a qualified electrician. At the very least, you will require armoured cable.

Heating mats

If you have no mains electricity supply to the green-house, use low-voltage heating mats on which to stand your propagators – a low-voltage wire can be run quite safely from a transformer plugged into a socket in the house.

Gravel flooring

Use gravel over trampled soil as a floor for the green-house: water will drain away easily and the floor can be watered with a weedkiller or disinfectant once a year to keep down any problems.

Snow blanket

Don't remove the snow lying on greenhouses and cold frames in the winter as it will provide valuable insulation.

Two-room greenhouse

A partition and internal door within a greenhouse will permit different conditions to be employed so that, for example, alpines could be grown at one end while warmth-requiring plants can occupy the other.

Ventilating cloches

Keep the ventilation on glass cloches open throughout the winter – the slight heat loss is more than compensated for by the lessening of disease problems.

Year round insulation

Leave bubble film insulation in the greenhouse all year round. Most gardening books advise you to use it for winter only but it will help to keep it cool in summer just as it keeps it warm in winter (although you will need to untie it partially in autumn in order to disinfect the greenhouse satisfactorily).

Most sunlight

The most efficient greenhouse shape for capturing sunlight is a dome, although it makes relatively inefficient use of the available floor area.

Light reflection

The inside wall of a lean-to greenhouse should be painted white to reflect the maximum amount of light and warmth into the house.

How many ventilators?

When calculating the number of ventilators that you need in a greenhouse, work on the basis that the total area of the vents should be approximately 15 per cent of the floor area.

Fresh air against Botrytis

Keep the greenhouse vents open in late summer to minimize the damage caused to tomatoes and other plants by *Botrytis* grey mould.

Space-saving staging

Use removable staging in the part of the greenhouse where you grow tomatoes in order to make the most efficient use of the space during the winter. Put it in place after you have removed the tomato crop in the autumn.

Whitefly inspection

Check overwintering plants in the greenhouse every week and swiftly remove any leaves or plants affected by whitefly in order to ensure that tomatoes and other new stock introduced in the spring remain pest-free.

Melons

When growing melons in a greenhouse, space is saved by training them upwards, but the fruit must be supported with nets.

Clean your glass

Keep greenhouse and cold frame glass clean. As a general guideline, glass that is just dirty enough to be remarked upon will probably cut down light transmission by about 40 per cent.

What kind of cold frame?

If you intend to raise melons and other tender crops in a cold frame, you will probably fare best with a glass-sided model. But simply for winter protection and hardening off, a frame with glass cover and wooden sides is better.

Cold frame base

The best base for a cold frame is firmed clinker which will allow moisture to drain away and is least likely to encourage algal growth and earthworm activity.

Glass not plastic

Although glass cloches are more expensive than plastic types, they retain heat better, are most robust when correctly anchored, and will give service for years.

Christmas rose cloche

Place a cloche over Christmas roses as the buds swell to protect them from the rain and bring them into bloom a little earlier.

Cold frame regime

Use the following regime for hardening off plants in the cold frame – in the first week, open it halfway in the daytime and close it at night; in the second week, open it fully in the daytime and halfway at night.

Cloche anchor

The easiest way to anchor cloches is by stretching a length of plastic-coated training wire over them and securing it in the soil on either side with metal, skewer-pattern tent pegs.

17

The pond

Where to put your pool

Always site a garden pool away from overhanging deciduous trees and where it will receive at least eight hours of sunshine per day.

Suitable design

Choose a pool to suit the garden setting. An informal pool with a bog garden round the edge is not really appropriate in a formal setting in a paved area: hard edges would be more in keeping here.

Toddler hazard

Don't have a pool in a garden with very young children: a toddler can drown in a very few centimetres of water.

How many fish?

When calculating the number of fish to stock your pool, reckon that you will need approximately 1 cm (½ in) of fish (excluding fins) for every 8 litres (2 gallons) of water.

Leak-proof lining

When constructing a garden pool, don't be tempted to line it with a normal polythene sheet which will tear fairly quickly. Buy purpose-made butyl rubber sheeting which should carry a long guarantee against leaking.

The idea of a pool lined with puddled clay appeals to many traditionally minded gardeners. This is certainly the time-honoured method of construction but be warned that it is difficult. You will need a high quality natural clay layer, about 30 cm (1 ft) thick and rammed very solidly.

Trouble-free fountain

The easiest and safest way to arrange a fountain in your garden pool is by using one of the low-voltage models – these operate through a transformer plugged into the nearest mains supply, needing only a low-voltage wire running to the pool itself.

Run your pool fountain through the winter to keep the water agitated and prevent ice from forming on the surface.

Icy shock

Don't smash the ice of a garden pool: the shock waves could injure the fish.

Drainpipe shelter

Put a length of ceramic drainpipe in the bottom of your pool to provide the fish with shelter from herons or other predators.

Gradual descent

When planting water plants, gradually move their containers over a period of a few weeks from shallow water into the depth to which they are best suited.

Keep pesticides out

Never use a pesticide in the vicinity of a pool, stream or other water course.

Keep fertilizers out

Never use manure, other organic matter or fertilizer (other than that specially sold for the purpose) in a garden pool.

If you have pots of plants close to the edge of a pool, move them away from the edge when applying liquid fertilizer – if it runs into the water, it may harm your fish and also encourage prolific growth of algae.

Oxygenators

Don't grow Canadian pondweed as an oxygenator in your garden pool, or you risk acquiring blanket weed which seems to favour growing over this plant. *Ceratophyllum* and *Myriophyllum* are much better oxygenators.

Leaf control

Use a fishing net regularly to remove leaves from the surface of the pool before they sink to the bottom.

Fish must wait

After planting a garden pool, wait three weeks for water and plants to settle down before introducing fish.

Fish in winter

Don't forget to feed the fish in your pool during mild periods in the winter when they become active.

Fish deterrent

After planting water plants in planting baskets, place a layer of gravel over the top of the soil to discourage fish from disturbing them.

Watch out for duckweed

Examine newly purchased aquatic plants very carefully for any signs of duckweed: once it is introduced into your pool, it will be impossible to eradicate.

Plant shelving

Construct a garden pool with ledges at various levels within it in order to be able to grow plants suited to different water depths.

Water-lilies

Be especially careful when choosing water-lilies to select a variety suited to the depth and area of your pool – some are extremely vigorous.

Cut off the dead heads of water-lily flowers before they sink out of sight. They are large, fleshy objects and when they decay, they add significantly to the fouling of pool water.

Plant-eating fish

Don't put bottom-living fish such as tench into a garden pool because they will cause havoc by uprooting and eating your water plants.

Fish fungus

Quite commonly, after new fish have been introduced into a pool, some of them may develop a white fungus disease on their scales. In a pool, unlike an aquarium, it really isn't practical to treat this chemically and, in my experience, it is much better to let nature take its course. You may lose a few fish but others seem to develop resistance and overcome the infection.

Go to the specialists

Most garden centres stock only a very limited range of water plants and you may therefore never see the great range that exists. When stocking a new pool, therefore, it will probably be worthwhile making a visit to a specialist aquatic gardening centre.

Herons

There is no absolutely certain way to keep herons away from a garden pool. I have never found artificial birds to be at all effective and netting is most unsightly. A single strand of wire positioned around the pool edge at a height of about 15 cm (6 in) is as reliable a deterrent as anything.

Overflow

When constructing a new pool, don't forget to install an overflow pipe. Otherwise, in areas of high winter rainfall, the water will be continually spilling over.

18

Pots, containers and ornaments

Ventilate your tubs

Make it a routine, several times a year, to prick over the soil surface in tubs and other containers in which long-term plants are grown. The soil soon develops a hard crust that prevents the easy penetration of air, water and nutrients.

Ornaments for steps

To break the visually hard line of steps, place small containers of plants at the sides of each tread.

Bigger is better

As a rule of thumb, you will find that a pot or other outdoor plant container holding less compost than a conventional plant pot 20 cm (8 in) in diameter will require watering with frustrating frequency in summer.

Mind your floor

If you live in an apartment block, check the weight restrictions on your floor before introducing large plant containers – remember that 1 cubic metre (yard) of compost weighs 1 tonne (2000 lbs).

Clay is better

Clay pots are almost always more effective than plastic ones: they permit a better soil-water-air relationship and are much less likely to lead to waterlogging.

Quick-change terracotta

Good quality ornamental terracotta pots are expensive. To make the best use of them, therefore, pot up your plants in cheap, plain terracotta pots and place these inside the good quality ones. In this way, you can remove plants as they fade and replace them with others while still displaying the same containers.

Concrete needs weathering

When using new concrete plant containers, do leave them outdoors for a few weeks to weather fully: some types of concrete contain setting agents that can be harmful to plants.

Do-it-yourself 'stone' trough

To make a simple and inexpensive trough garden, cover an old sink with hypertufa (a mixture by volume of one part sharp sand, one part cement and two parts moss peat, stirred with water into a thick 'porridge'). When it hardens, it will closely simulate the appearance of rock.

Hanging baskets

For hanging baskets, use a specially formulated compost containing a water-retentive gel to help minimize the amount of watering required.

Before putting up a hanging basket, be sure that the

bracket is well secured and capable of bearing the weight.

When choosing fuchsias for hanging baskets, remember that while the upright-growing varieties are ideal as centrepieces, you will need the pendulous forms (now sometimes called basket fuchsias) for the sides.

Use small climbing plants such as *Thunbergia* in hanging baskets and allow them to grow *upwards* and cover the chains.

Quick-change window box

For window boxes, make a wooden container to fit on the window sill, line it with plastic sheet and make a few drainage holes inside, then fill it with pots of plants rather than planting directly into the box. In this way, it will be easy to change the planting arrangements as different types of plant come into flower during the course of the season.

Pot-hole planting

When setting up a hanging basket, parsley pot or other container where plants are to emerge through holes in the sides, insert the plants through the holes from within as the container is filled with compost. If you try to push them in later from the outside, they will invariably be damaged.

Half-barrels

Wooden half-barrels are among the cheapest of the really large types of plant container. To lengthen their lives, line them with plastic sheets so that the compost does not come into direct contact with the wood – but do remember to make drainage holes in the bottom of both the plastic and the barrel.

Unless they are being used for very large, long-term plants such as trees, it is not usually necessary to fill completely a half-barrel or other very large container with expensive compost. Half-fill it with a mixture of garden soil and rocks and then top this up with compost which will thus provide a perfectly adequate rooting depth.

Moving heavy containers

When using large plant containers such as wooden half-barrels, try to position them in their intended final sites before filling them. If they do have to be moved when full, lengths of old scaffolding pipe are among the few things that are strong yet manageable enough to use as rollers.

Go for groups

Group together containers of varying sizes for maximum effect: they almost always look better than odd ones. But try to keep the types (terracotta, wood and so forth) consistent within each group.

Rustic pots

For most attractive rustic containers, use lengths of old hollow tree trunk, lined with plastic sheet. It is often possible to pick up such timber very cheaply at timber yards or suppliers of logs for burning.

Don't crack your pots

When stacking terracotta pots, especially large ones, place a couple of sheets of newspaper between them. This will prevent the pots from jamming together and possibly being cracked.

19

The lawn

When to lay or sow

Although lawns can be laid or sown at any time of the year when the weather isn't frosty or very dry, the two best months are generally April and September.

Suitable site

Don't make the mistake of believing that the site for a lawn must be dead flat: a gently sloping or undulating lawn is most attractive. Avoid, however, having humps and hollows so acute that they will be scraped by the mower.

Avoid meadow turf

When buying turf for a lawn, always choose specially grown turf, not meadow turf which has been cut from fields and invariably contains weeds. The designation 'weed-treated' means nothing and offers no certainty that any weeds have actually been killed.

Suitable grass seed

When buying grass seed or lawn turf, be sure to choose a blend of grasses that is appropriate for your needs: rye grasses are hard-wearing and will stand up to normal traffic whereas mixtures without rye grass will give the finest possible velvet sward.

Laying turf

When laying turves, do not place a short piece at the end of a row where it will fray; move a large piece to the end and insert the short piece next to it.

When laying a new lawn, always work from a wooden plank in order to avoid damage to the turves.

Remember that when lawn turf is delivered, it will be in rolls. These are very heavy so should be dropped as close as possible to where they will be needed; and they should be laid as soon as possible, for the grass will begin to yellow after about five days.

Lifting turf

When lifting turf, use a fork to tear it up, not a spade which severs the roots.

Improved drainage

To improve the drainage on your lawn, hire (they are too costly to justify buying) a powered hollow-tine lawn spiker which removes plugs of soil.

Cylinder is best

For the best possible finish on a fine lawn, use a cylinder rather than a rotary mower.

Most beautiful mowing

For the most effective mowing and most attractive appearance, mow lawns twice in directions at 90° to each other. The most striking effect of all is achieved when the lawn is mown in this way with a cylinder mower, diagonally to the point of view.

Rake in seed

After sowing a lawn, lightly rake the seed into the soil rather than leaving it exposed on the surface where it will germinate much less satisfactorily.

Economize on feeding

To save time and money on lawn care, forget about the liquid summer green-up feeds and concentrate on spring and autumn feeds only.

The finest lawn edge

For the finest lawn edge, use a specially designed half-moon lawn-edging knife rather than a spade, and slope the tool outwards to avoid the edge crumbling when it is trodden on.

Good old-fashioned weeding

For a small lawn, with few deep-rooted weeds, don't bother with chemical controls but use a V-shaped daisy grubber instead – an old-fashioned tool but one that is still extremely useful.

Wear and tear

To minimize grass wear and tear at the places where you step on to the lawn, peg down heavy duty plastic netting – it is available specially for the purpose. As the grass grows, the net will disappear into the turf but still provide support in the soil to prevent damage.

Rollers are out

Never use a roller on your lawn: they almost invariably create or at least accentuate humps and hollows rather than correcting them, and they compact the turf like nothing else does.

Weedkiller on lawns

Don't use weedkiller on the spring lawn until the weather is warm and the soil moist.

Be kind to worms

Avoid using lawn fertilizers containing worm killers. Worms are beneficial to a lawn and will save you much hard work in spiking and aeration.

Grasses hate shade

Don't try to establish grasses beneath the shade of large trees. They will never grow there satisfactorily and you will constantly be plagued with bare patches, weeds and moss.

Winter lawnmowing

Don't be afraid to mow your lawn in winter if it continues to grow through mild spells – but be sure to set the cutters high.

Keep off frozen grass

Don't walk on the lawn when the grass is frozen: you will break the grass blades and leave brown marks that will persist until the spring.

Teabag repairs

Make repair patches for your lawn by sowing grass seeds on damp, used teabags.

Bird deterrent

Protect newly sown lawns from birds by stretching lightweight fruit-cage netting over the area, supported on upturned plastic plant pots on top of bamboo canes.

Electric lawn rake

When using an electric lawn rake, take off the collector box which is invariably too small, use the appliance without it and rake the moss and thatch into heaps with a normal spring-tine lawn rake.

Curved lawn edge

To define a curved edge when cutting turf to form the edge of a lawn, lay a hosepipe on the ground and either fix the pipe with pairs of canes or leave it in place for a few days – the grass will turn yellow and clearly indicate the line where you need to cut.

Filling in cracks

After a period of drought, large cracks will form on lawns, especially on clayey soils. Brush a mixture of soil and grit with a scattering of bonemeal into them. This will not only fill the gaps but also help to improve the drainage.

Lawn surgery

To remedy small humps and hollows in your lawn, cut H-shaped slots in the turf with a lawn-edging knife, peel back the pieces at the sides and then add or remove soil. To aid re-establishment of the grass, mix a small amount of bonemeal with the infilling soil.

Where lawn meets wall

Where a lawn edge abuts a vertical surface – a kerb or low wall for instance – cut a channel about 5 cm (2 in) wide between the two. You will have some extra edge-trimming to do but the effect will be very much better than if you try to mow up to the vertical, when at best you will be left with tufts of grass and at worst you may damage your mower.

Recycled turf

Never throw away old turf that you have stripped from a lawn or other grassy area. Stack it upside-down, cover it with a heavy duty black plastic sheet and it will rot down to leave a high quality, organic rich, compost-making loam.

Edge repairs

To repair a broken edge of a lawn, cut a square of turf round the broken portion, turn it so that the broken part faces inwards and re-lay it. You will then have a firm edge while the damaged part may be packed with compost and seeded.

Cut out weeds

The only effective way to remove patches of weed grass species from a lawn is to dig them out and re-turf the bare areas – ideally after killing the patch with a non-persistent weedkiller.

Dressing a new lawn

Use autumn lawn fertilizer as a base dressing when sowing or laying a new lawn.

Trouble with chamomile

Try a chamomile lawn only if you have light, well-drained soil, a sunny position and you are prepared to spend a good deal of time hand-weeding.

When to mow a meadow

Do not cut a wildflower meadow until late in the summer and certainly not until the seeds have begun to ripen. Then allow the cuttings to lie on the ground to dry, just as farmers do with hay. In this way, all of the seeds will be shed and annual species will regenerate themselves satisfactorily.

Wildflower meadows

An area of about 100 sq m (yds) is the minimum on which a self-perpetuating wildflower meadow can effectively be created.

20

Trees

How deep?

To get an idea of the spread of a tree's root system, it is reasonable to work on the basis that it will be as far underground as the crown is above.

How high?

To determine the height of a tree, cut a piece of stick the same length as the distance from your eye to your outstretched fist. Then hold the stick by its centre, vertically at arm's length, and move backwards and forwards, sighting the stick on the tree. When the top and bottom of the stick coincide with the top and bottom of the tree, mark the point on the ground. The distance from this spot to the tree is a close approximation of the tree's height.

Planting hints

When planting trees and shrubs, be sure to spread the roots carefully in the planting hole. This will help ensure better establishment and a more stable plant.

When planting a tree or shrub, shake the plant up and down in the planting hole as you fill it with soil. In this way, you will ensure that the soil fills all the gaps round the roots and leaves no air pockets where water may accumulate and stagnate.

Watch out for fungus

If you find a bracket-shaped fungal growth emerging from the trunk of a tree, especially at some distance from the ground, be warned. There will almost certainly be extensive decay within the wood which could render the tree unstable and liable to blow down in a gale.

Weed-free zone

Always keep an area about 1 m (3 ft) in diameter close to a newly planted young tree free from weeds. Although the tree will be robust enough when mature, it is no more capable of competing effectively with weed growth than any other small plant.

Honey fungus

After cutting down a deciduous tree, try to remove the stump or have it ground out. At the very least, cover it with soil as the cut surface can provide an entry point for honey fungus to establish itself in your garden.

Preserve your trees

Never cut down an existing tree or large shrub until you have been in a new garden for at least nine months and so gained an idea of the importance that the plant has for privacy, shade and shelter.

If your house lies in a designated conservation area, be careful before you cut down any trees (other than those diseased or dangerous). In general, any tree in

101

such an area has automatic legal protection if it exceeds 75 cm (30 in) (or, in some instances, 100 cm (40 in)) in diameter at 1.5 m (5 ft) above soil level. Take advice if you are in any doubt.

Trees and the law

You are perfectly entitled to cut branches off a neighbour's tree that overhangs your garden; but legally you are obliged to offer him the material that you cut off.

Rogue shoots

If plain, green-leaved shoots arise on variegated trees and shrubs, prune them out. They will be more vigorous than the variegated shoots and will eventually take over the plant.

Safe ties

When attaching a belt-style tie to secure a tree to a stake, be sure to fix the buckle adjacent to the stake, not to the tree, which will be damaged by it.

Check the ties on fast-growing trees and shrubs at least once a year – rapid growth in girth can result in the plant strangling itself.

When using wire to tie up or support the branches of trees or large shrubs, slip a short length of old hosepipe over the wire where it is in contact with the branch to prevent damage.

Rogue buds

To form an attractive standard tree, especially one with ornamental bark, be sure to rub out any buds that form low down on the trunk.

Dead or alive

A simple test to ascertain if a leafless twig is alive is to scratch a small part with a fingernail. If bright green tissue shows, it is alive; if brown tissue, dead; and if dirty green, moribund.

Best value

Overall, the best and most versatile tree for small gardens is the white-blossomed *Amelanchier lamarckii*, which is tolerant both of clay soil and strong winds.

Brighten up your evergreens

Relatively dull and monotonous evergreen trees and shrubs can be brought to life by training flowering climbers through them. Clematis are good for long-term permanent plantings, but for quick summer colour the orange-and-red-flowered climbing nasturtiums, grown from seed, are superb.

Beautiful but brittle

Do not plant the common ornamental trees *Gleditsia triacanthos* 'Sunburst' or *Robinia pseudoacacia* 'Frisia' in a windy position: their brittle twigs will be prone to damage.

Tie in your conifers

Use strong training wire to tie in the vertical branches of columnar conifers. Even after relatively light snowfalls, they will otherwise open outwards like peeled bananas.

Avoid Kanzan

When planting ornamental cherries, avoid the common double pink-flowered 'Kanzan' which has been subject to a mysterious disease in recent years; many mature and established trees have died.

Unusual mountain ash

To add unusual variety to trees of mountain ash type, select the orange-yellow-fruited *Sorbus* 'Joseph Rock' or the white-fruited *S. hupehensis*.

Japanese maples

Do not plant ornamental Japanese maples in a position where they will be subjected to waterlogged soil or strong winds.

Holly

If you want a holly bush to produce berries, be sure to buy a female plant – some named varieties are solely male.

Throw some netting over a branch of a berrying holly tree in late November to be sure that the birds leave you a few berries for Christmas.

Evergreen shelter

If you plant evergreens in autumn, erect a screen of hessian or plastic netting to protect them from the cold through their first winter.

Keep poplars away from apples

Never plant poplars as windbreaks round apple orchards as they can harbour canker disease.

Early delivery

If tree and shrub plants ordered by mail are delivered while the soil is frozen, open the top of their packaging only and keep them in a shed or garage until the weather warms up again.

Winter blossom

For a reliable winter-blooming tree, try the winter-flowering cherry. If you cut sprigs to bring indoors at any time during the winter, they can be guaranteed to burst into flower.

Winter colour

For the best and most vivid red winter stem colour among dogwoods, choose the 'Westonbirt' form of *Cornus alba* 'Sibirica'.

Don't move magnolias

More than most types of tree, magnolias resent root disturbance and it is especially important therefore to choose their positions carefully – moving a large plant generally results in its demise.

21

Shrubs

Encourage new roots

When planting shrubs, especially deciduous types, tipping back the shoots will help encourage the formation of masses of new fibrous roots.

Rhododendrons

Plant rhododendrons and azaleas shallowly: deep planting is one of the commonest reasons for failure of these plants.

Winner in the worst corner

For the most difficult, dry and shady corner of the garden, there is no better plant than *Aucuba japonica*, the spotted laurel; the variety 'Crotonifolia' has the best leaf colour although 'Variegata', a female strain, bears red berries too.

Long-lasting fuchsia

One of the flowering shrubs with the longest period in bloom is the hardy fuchsia 'Mrs Popple'.

Frost-free fuchsias

In autumn, mound compost round the crowns of outdoor fuchsias or other slightly tender plants in order to give them some protection from penetrating frost.

Giant-flowered wisteria

For the longest flower trusses on a wisteria (sometimes up to 1 m (3 ft) in length), select the variety 'Macrobotrys' (also called 'Multijuga').

How safe are your walls?

Don't plant self-clinging climbers such as ivy on old crumbly bricks or mortar; they will be perfectly safe however on sound masonry or brickwork.

Blue hydrangeas

Add proprietary blueing powder to the soil to produce blue hydrangea flowers on alkaline soil.

Actinidia needs warmth

To obtain the best leaf coloration on the attractive climber *Actinidia kolomikta*, it must be planted against a warm wall and, even then, only in the early part of the summer and when the plant is well established will the variegation be seen at its best.

Clematis hints

For the best orange colour among the late-summer-flowering clematis species, choose *Clematis tangutica* 'Bill Mackenzie'.

When planting new clematis, plant them about 10–15 cm (4–6 in) deeper than the soil mark on the stem base to lessen the chances of them being affected by wilt disease.

Grow the less vigorous varieties of clematis in a mixed border and peg down some of their shoots so they produce a mound of growth covered in blooms.

For extra flowering appeal, plant clematis at the base of climbing roses – but choose varieties that are not too vigorous and have complementary colours.

For the best flower colour on many of the early large-flowered hybrid clematis like 'Nelly Moser', plant them on a north wall where they will not be bleached by the sun.

For an unusual spring-flowering clematis of fairly restricted growth, try the various forms of bell-flowered *Clematis alpina*, especially the large blue 'Frances Rivis' or the double 'White Moth'.

Best Virginia creeper

The best ornamental self-clinging vine of 'Virginia creeper' type is *Parthenocissus tricuspidata* 'Veitchii', also called *Ampelopsis veitchii*.

Flowering tree

To create an attractive small flowering tree, train a wisteria by twining its shoots round a central post to form a standard.

Frost-free hydrangeas

Leave the dead shoots on hydrangeas, outdoor fuchsias and similar slightly tender shrubs during the winter to provide added frost protection. Cut them off in the spring.

Colourful late climber

For an unusual and vigorous climbing plant for late autumn and winter appeal try *Celastrus orbiculatus* hermaphrodite form, which has brown fruits that split open in autumn to reveal yellow interiors and red seeds. The hermaphrodite form is essential to obtain satisfactory fruit set.

Fragrant evergreen

For a lovely evergreen small shrub with winter interest, try the rarely seen and delightfully perfumed *Sarcococca confusa*.

Honeysuckle

Plant climbing honeysuckles in the more wild parts of the garden where they can climb over old tree stumps, fence posts or up into living trees. Their straggly, loose habit is never satisfactorily contained on a formal trellis or house wall.

Unusual scrambler

For an unusual and very vigorous scrambling plant for the wilder garden, try the double-flowered bramble *Rubus ulmifolius* 'Bellidiflorus'.

Prettiest mound

One of the prettiest, deciduous mound-forming or ground-cover shrubs is *Stephanandra incisa* 'Crispa'.

Ceanothus

Ceanothus are among the few really striking blue-flowered shrubs; remember that the spring- and early-summer-blooming evergreen types are less hardy than the late-summer- and autumn-blooming deciduous forms.

Winter jasmine

To obtain a neat, hedge-like appearance against a wall, winter jasmine should be clipped fairly hard in the first half of April.

Ivy

It is almost impossible to encourage ivy to climb until it is ready to do so. Plant it in the chosen position therefore and wait: some varieties will form a rounded mound of growth for a couple of years and then begin to climb when they are ready.

Forsythia

The best flowering variety of forsythia is the old, golden yellow 'Spectabilis'.

Lilacs

Lilacs are very pretty in flower but should not be chosen for small gardens as their foliage is dull in the extreme, they grow very large and exhaust the soil's nutrients, and the blossom browns most unattractively as it fades.

Mock orange

The most compact among the mock oranges and the most suitable for smaller gardens is *Philadelphus* 'Manteau d'hermine'.

22

Roses

Climbers beat ramblers

For the longest flowering period and freedom from disease, choose climbing rather than rambling varieties.

Replant disease

When replanting an old rose bed with new stock, there is always a risk of the plants failing to establish satisfactorily because of rose replant disease. Either leave the soil free from roses for two years or dig out a hole of about 30 cm (1 ft) cube for each plant and refill it with soil taken from another part of the garden.

Painless roses

If you want a climbing rose close to a doorway or path, and you are worried about the prickles, grow the thornless climber 'Zephirine Drouhin'.

Pegging climbers

Bend and peg the shoots of climbing roses down to slightly below the horizontal to encourage flowering along their entire length.

Pruning

Do not carry out any autumn pruning on those shrub rose varieties that bear attractive hips.

Minimize spraying

Use a combined insecticide and fungicide treatment on roses to avoid having to spray more often than necessary.

The rule of three

Prune floribunda roses by the rule of three – remove completely the oldest one third of the shoots and cut back the remainder by one third.

The rule of two

Prune hybrid tea roses by the rule of two – cut back all shoots by about one half – slightly less for strong growing varieties, slightly more for weaker ones.

Minimize pruning

If you like roses but are less than enthusiastic about pruning, why not choose some of the lower growing shrub varieties: they may flower for a shorter period than the bush roses, but they are much easier to care for.

Roses love moisture

Although roses succeed admirably on a clay soil, it is not the clay itself that is the secret of success, it is moisture retentiveness. Even a light sandy soil can be rendered suitable for rose-growing by the addition of copious amounts of organic matter.

Black spot free

There are few bush yellow roses reliably resistant to black spot: among the best are 'Grandpa Dickson' (hybrid tea), 'Allgold', 'Arthur Bell' and 'Korresia' (floribundas).

Rain tolerant

In very wet areas, try the low-growing, single pink-flowered shrub rose 'Ballerina' which is remarkably rain tolerant.

Leaf-rolling sawfly

The tightly rolled appearance of rose leaves is a result of attack by the leaf-rolling sawfly, but unlike most pest symptoms the effects arise even if the insects have laid no eggs on the leaf. Consequently, removing all of the damaged foliage, as is often suggested, may well have no effect.

Living mulch

The soil under established roses can look very bare when the roses themselves aren't in bloom. Why not try the William Robinson technique of growing a 'living mulch' of violets beneath? But do remember that a little extra feeding will be needed to compensate for the competition that the roses will experience.

Budding roses

When budding roses, be sure to keep the buds moist during the time between cutting them from the parent plant and inserting them on to the rootstock.

How to avoid suckers

To avoid the problem of rose suckers, take cuttings from your plants in late autumn. Use 25 cm (10 in) lengths of woody shoots of the current year's growth and insert them 15 cm (6 in) deep in a shady corner of the garden. The resulting bushes will be growing on their own roots and all shoots will therefore be of the flowering variety.

How to dead-head

When dead-heading roses, cut the stem back to a point just above the first leaf bearing five, not three, leaflets.

Ground cover

Don't forget roses when choosing ground-cover plants. There are several very attractive low-growing varieties including the pale pink 'Nozomi' and the white 'Swany'.

Single-flowered hybrid teas

Among the most attractive yet least known among rose varieties are the single-flowered hybrid teas such as 'Dainty Bess' and 'White Wings'. They were very popular between the wars but are still available.

Tough enough for hedging

The toughest of all rose varieties and suitable for hedging even in fairly exposed areas are the hybrid rugosas such as 'Blanc Double de Coubert'.

Order your standards early

If standard roses appeal to you, then remember that the demand for them always exceeds supply so you will need to order well in advance from nurseries. This is especially true of the most attractive of all, the weeping standards, usually formed by grafting a rambler variety on to a standard rootstock.

Stimulate new roots

When planting new, bare-root roses, trim back the roots by about one third to stimulate the formation of new fibrous roots and so provide firm anchorage.

Tripod support

The most reliable way of providing support for the large, spreading shrub rose varieties is by erecting a stout tripod of wooden stakes, braced near to the top by cross pieces.

Wet weather problem

Don't be unduly concerned if the flowers on some of your roses fail to open properly in very wet weather. This is a condition called balling and is an unavoidable problem on some thinner-petalled varieties.

Robins' pincushions

Woolly, reddish growths on rose stems are called robins' pincushions. They are the results of the activity of a sawfly but are not harmful. If they are very unsightly, simply cut them off.

New ways with bush roses

Many people dislike modern bush roses but I am sure that this is due to them so often being seen massed together in a wide range of colours. Used in groups of three or four of single colours, either alone or, better still, among other plants in a border, they can be useful and valuable. And, in this way, you will avoid that stark twiggy appearance in winter.

Most beautiful prickles

For something unusual try growing the rose with the largest and most beautiful prickles of all, the shrub variety called *Rosa sericea pteracantha*.

Protecting roses from wind damage

All types of rose are likely to produce a few abnormally long shoots and even if these are required to form part of the plant's permanent framework, they should be shortened by about a third and, if necessary, tied in, in the late autumn before they are whipped around by winter winds.

Frost hollows

Rose bushes are rather prone to being moved in the ground by the wind, so creating a small hollow at the base of the stem. This should be filled in with soil and the plant carefully firmed. Otherwise, rainwater will collect in the hollow and then freeze, so causing damage to the stem tissues.

23

Perennials

Planning a border

When planning a herbaceous border, bear in mind that it is difficult to accommodate sufficient plants to achieve anything approaching continuity of flower through the season with a bed much less than 5–8 m (15–25 ft) long and 2 m (6 ft) deep.

For the most attractive colour blend in a herbaceous border, follow Gertrude Jekyll's maxim and keep the hot, fiery colours to the centre with the more pastel shades to the sides.

New border

When planting a new mixed or shrub border, make use of annuals to fill in the gaps, until the larger plants have matured.

Plant herbaceous and bedding plants in groups of three or five to achieve a more rapid and effective display.

Simple support

For the easiest, most efficient and inconspicuous method of giving support to herbaceous perennials, use

L-shaped interlocking supports of plastic-covered wire.

Install stakes or other supports for herbaceous perennials when they are about 20–30 cm (8–12 in) tall. If you leave them until they are much taller than this you will be likely to damage their stems.

Autumn gold

For easy and reliable border perennials to give rich golden-and-yellow-coloured autumn flowers, try growing heleniums.

Butterfly attraction

Plant *Buddleia davidii*, *Sedum spectabile*, thymes and Michaelmas daisies to attract butterflies to the garden.

Foxgloves

To maintain a white population of foxgloves, pull out any plants with pink flowers before their blooms actually open: this will prevent any cross pollination occurring.

The common species of foxgloves are short-lived. For something different, why not try some of the perennial types? My own favourite is the orange-and-brown-flowered *Digitalis laevigata*.

Lavender

To cut lavender for dried use indoors, don't wait until the flowers fade. Cut them just after the blooms have passed their peak – in this way, the perfume will be retained.

Paeonies

Move paeony plants just as growth is beginning in spring and do so with the minimum possible disturbance to the large, fleshy tubers. In this way, you will be less likely to lose a season's flowers.

Delphiniums

In windy gardens, traditional, tall-stemmed delphiniums can be a frustrating disappointment. Instead, therefore, try such shorter growing varieties as 'Blue Tit' (dark blue) or 'Mighty Atom' (lilac).

When delphiniums begin to shoot in the spring, remove weak and spindly shoots to leave four or five only per plant.

Sweet peas

If you have neither time nor inclination to grow sweet peas annually from seed, try the perennial species *Lathyrus latifolius* or *L. grandiflorus*.

Ground cover

A valuable, although slightly aggressive, ground-cover plant for the wilder parts of the garden is the native dwarf meadow rue, *Thalictrum minus*, which has foliage reminiscent of the maidenhair fern and tiny yellow flowers.

Pampas grass

The traditional types of pampas grass are far too large for most modern gardens and you will fare much better with the 1.5 m (5 ft) tall 'Sunningdale Silver'.

Red hot pokers

Kniphofias (red hot pokers) are among the least hardy of the common herbaceous perennials. They are best given winter protection by drawing up their evergreen foliage and tying it loosely over the top of the plant to guard against frost damage.

Thin out late bloomers

In late spring, thin out the shoots on late-summer-flowering herbaceous perennials such as Michaelmas daisies to obtain a stronger, better display of flowers.

Mildew-free daisies

The best Michaelmas daisy varieties to grow if you are plagued with mildew are those derived from *Aster novae-angliae*, *A. × frikartii* and *A. × thompsonii*.

Ligularia

Among the most striking plants for a moist border in late summer are the various species and varieties of *Ligularia*; but bear in mind that with their large leaves, they will be the first to wilt in dry conditions.

Lupins

If lupins are to your liking, then the best varieties to grow are the modern 'New Generation Hybrids', but you should be aware that in most parts of the country all lupins will be severely attacked by the very large lupin aphid, a recent arrival in this country from North America.

Astrantia

A very useful border perennial for a slightly shaded and damp situation is *Astrantia*, which has the added advantage of flowers that are most attractive when dried.

Japanese invasion

A lovely plant for the autumn border is the Japanese anemone (the white varieties especially) but it can be invasive so shouldn't be planted where this is likely to cause problems.

Angel's fishing rod

The wand flower or angel's fishing rod (*Dierama*) is a graceful plant for late summer but many gardeners have difficulty with it as they forget that it is evergreen and its foliage must not be cut back at the end of the season.

Aquilegias

Stout-stemmed perennials that require no staking are always valuable if you are looking for a low maintenance garden. Aquilegias are among the best of these for spring flowering.

Silver leaves in the sun

In a dry, sunny spot, you will generally succeed best with silvery-leaved plants, those of Mediterranean origin, or seaside plants which often have the specific name *maritima* or *maritimum*.

Best value, but . . .

Among the most reliable, easy, long-lived and floriferous among lower growing perennials are the many species and varieties of hardy geranium. Their drawback is that most types need support and a few are notorious at self-seeding.

Carnations and pinks

If you admire carnations but have no heated greenhouse or the time to raise perpetual varieties, the hardy border carnation makes a very good substitute. They will require support if they are not to lie flat on the ground.

When staking border carnations, be sure that the support still allows the flower head to flop slightly. This is its natural habit and prevents rain from collecting in the head and spoiling it.

Don't attempt to support garden pinks: they have a naturally loose habit that can't be corrected.

Replace pinks and border carnations every four years with fresh stock.

Himalayan blue poppies

The so-called Himalayan blue poppies of the genus *Meconopsis* are among the most sought-after border plants, but they are not always easy to grow, one of the problems being that most are monocarpic – they die after flowering. To avoid losing a good flowering strain such as those in the *M.* × *sheldonii* crosses, remove the flowering spikes from a few of the shoots each year before they elongate. In this way, while parts of the clump may die, others will continue.

24

Annuals and biennials

Wallflowers

To establish plants such as wallflowers most readily in the crevices of walls, use seed rather than transplants. Mix the seed with a soil-based potting compost and push it into the nooks and crannies. Many annual or biennial species will self-seed subsequently.

Sow seeds of wallflowers and other biennials for next year within a month of the flowers fading on this year's plants.

Wallflowers are popular for spring colour but bear in mind that to raise your own, you will need plenty of room; they are large plants and must be sown into a seed bed (which they will occupy for several months) in early summer and then transplanted into their flowering positions in autumn.

Storing pelargoniums

Store pelargoniums in a frost-free place in large envelopes, each made from an entire newspaper. Cut the top growth down to about 20 cm (8 in) and remove the largest leaves first.

All-weather petunias

Petunias are lovely for summer colour but can be devastated in cold wet weather. For the best success in all summers, select the 'Resisto' range of varieties.

Selectable stocks

To obtain double-flowered stocks, always choose those varieties labelled as 'selectable'; by reducing the temperature after germination, you will induce the potentially double-flowered plants to reveal themselves by their paler leaves.

Sweet peas

After sweet pea seedlings have produced three pairs of leaves, pinch out the top to encourage bushy growth and plenty of flowers.

Cut sweet pea flowers regularly: once some are allowed to set seed, the flowering of the plant overall declines markedly.

Sweet peas can be sown in autumn or very early in the spring but autumn sowing is only really worthwhile if you intend to grow plants of exhibition quality.

Divine perfume

To bring the most delectable perfume into your flower beds, sow a few mignonette seeds among other plants. Visually, they have nothing special to commend them but the scent is divine.

Be extravagant with annuals

Whether you raise your own summer bedding plants or buy them, don't be too economical. A few plants may well fail to establish or fall prey to pests and diseases. Gaps in formal plantings can look dreadful so always keep a few plants in reserve.

White lobelia

When growing white varieties of lobelia, always remember that no truly all-white strain exists and you will need to weed out the few blue-flowered plants that inevitably arise.

Container daisy

One of the loveliest and daintiest annuals for growing in containers is *Brachycome*, the Swan river daisy, which has soft feathery foliage and dainty, scented, daisy-like flowers in white, pink or purple.

Aster wilt

Asters commonly fail because of a soil-inhabiting disease called aster wilt which builds up in soil where asters have been grown previously. Its effects can be avoided by raising the plants individually in 9 cm (3½ in) pots of compost and then planting them out in the undisturbed pot ball.

Various busy lizzies

For extra variety among busy lizzies, choose from the 'New Guinea Hybrids' which combine many large flowers with attractively patterned foliage.

Order plantlets early

If you have difficulty in raising bedding plants from seed (or simply don't have the room), remember that most seed companies now offer a range of plantlets (small plants ready for pricking on) but demand always exceeds supply so do order them early.

Poor man's orchid

In general, you will achieve the most striking effects by planting up pots and containers with bedding plants of single-coloured varieties but among those with which mixed colours can be particularly attractive is *Schizanthus* or poor man's orchid.

Sweet williams

When sowing wallflowers, don't forget those other delightful garden biennials, sweet williams, which have unaccountably fallen from popularity. They should be grown and treated in exactly the same way as wallflowers.

Mexican sunflower

Most annuals are inevitably fairly small plants but one attractive and generally unappreciated exception is *Tithonia*, the Mexican sunflower which makes a bushy plant about 1 m (3 ft) tall with rich orange, daisy-like flowers.

Lobelia in a strawberry pot

For a striking addition to your summer bedding plant display, use a terracotta strawberry pot for growing lobelia. Before long, the whole will be covered with a dense mass of blue flowers.

Black carnation

There are few annuals with flowers that can truly be said to be black. One of the closest is a striking plant, the annual carnation 'Black and White Minstrels', that has picotee flowers of the very deepest purple and white, which will bring a great deal of interest to the garden in late summer.

Everlasting flowers

Not many annuals are of especial value for flower arranging but among those that should always be in a flower arranger's garden are the everlasting flowers such as *Dimorphotheca*, the ornamental annual grasses and the curious, green-flowered bells of Ireland, *Molucella*.

Lavatera

One of the most stunning and successful new annuals of recent years is the rich pink-flowered lavatera called 'Silver Cup', a plant that should be in every collection of border annuals.

Don't fertilize nasturtiums

Nasturtiums are traditional summer garden annuals with a range of bright shades of red, yellow and orange flowers, but do remember that the poorer the soil, the more flowers you will have. Give them fertilizer and you will only have foliage.

Pansies

Undoubtedly, the best annuals for providing colour in the garden through the winter and into the spring are winter-flowering or universal pansies but they really must have a sunny position to give their best.

The large-flowered varieties of summer-blooming pansy are not to everyone's taste but they have several close relatives with very much smaller, dainty blooms. The pale blue 'Baby Lucia' and the dark purple 'Prince Henry' are two of my favourites.

Evening perfume

A number of annuals are especially valuable for offering perfume late in the evening. Among the best of these are ornamental tobacco (*Nicotiana*) and night-scented stocks.

More or less orange

The large-flowered African, French and Afro-French marigolds provide the biggest boldest display of orange flowers but if they are too assertive for your taste, you might prefer their smaller relatives, tagetes.

Carpet bedding

If you have admired the carpet bedding schemes in public parks and wish to reproduce them in your own garden, remember that they depend for their effect on rather special types of plant grown not for their flowers but their foliage which must be trimmed back during the season. Seed is available from seed companies but a greenhouse will be required to raise the plants.

Rust-free antirrhinums

Antirrhinums have long been favourites but in recent years they have been devastated by rust disease. If you are choosing varieties for the garden, therefore, be sure to select only those specifically listed as rust resistant.

Taller than lizzy

If you enjoy busy lizzies, you might also wish to try their less common and taller growing relatives, generally sold simply as *Impatiens* or camellia-flowered *impatiens*.

Sun-loving daisies

Because it is impossible to predict summer weather, don't rely too heavily on daisies such as gazanias and zinnias which come from warm dry climates when choosing your summer annuals. They undoubtedly give a wonderful show in warm dry summers but in wet seasons are greatly disappointing.

Blue salvias

Even if the brilliant red-flowered salvias are not to your taste, you may well appreciate their dark-blue-flowered relatives like *Salvia farinacea* for late summer.

Gap fillers

Don't forget that annuals can be very useful to fill in gaps in herbaceous borders and other more permanent plantings. It is always worth growing or buying a few extra plants for this purpose therefore.

25

Bulbs, corms and rhizomes

Planting bulbs

Always plant bulbs so that the soil above the bulb is equivalent to twice its overall height.

Plant bulbs in groups of the same variety: if you plant mixtures, the later flowering types will bear their blooms among the dying heads of the earlier ones, so lessening their impact.

When planting bulbs, lay them on about 2 cm (1 in) depth of sand to which a scattering of bonemeal has been added. This will minimize rotting and aid root establishment.

When planting bulbs for naturalizing beneath turf, lift 30 cm (1 ft) squares of turf and plant groups of bulbs beneath each square, rather than trying to plant them individually.

Marking spring bulbs

Use small canes to mark the position of spring-flowering bulbs before they fade, otherwise you may disturb or damage them when summer planting.

Pretty but wild

Some common ornamental plants are notoriously vigorous and invasive yet on the other hand so pretty that one really can't be without them. My advice is not to plant such types in a border but grow them instead in a fairly wild part of the garden where they can be allowed freer rein. Top of my list for this approach are bluebells, Japanese anemones, some of the ground-smothering geraniums, like 'Claridge Druce', and lily of the valley.

Daffodils

Don't knot the foliage of daffodils: it impairs their functioning – and looks terrible.

To multiply your valuable daffodil stock, cut some bulbs into four pieces, soak them for half an hour in a solution of benomyl fungicide, incubate them at room temperature for about 12 weeks and then pot them up. They should flower in two or three years.

For the earliest daffodil flowers, two of the most reliable types are the tiny hoop-petticoat *Narcissus bulbocodium conspicuus* or the more conventionally bloomed 'February Gold'.

Cyclamen for winter

To take over when the common *Cyclamen hederifolium* finishes flowering in autumn, plant the less frequently seen winter- and spring-blooming *C. coum atkinsii*.

Growing from seed

If raising bulbous plants from seed, plan on having to wait on average three or four years before they bloom.

Colchicums

Colchicums or naked ladies are very attractive bulbs but
their flower stems are almost invariably so weak that
they flop over in an unsightly manner. Always plant
them among unmown grass or other fairly tall vegetation, therefore, to give them support.

Nerines

Plant nerine bulbs just below the surface – rather like
shallots, with the tops poking through.

Shallow lily

Alone among lilies, *Lilium candidum*, the Madonna lily,
should be planted just below the surface; others require
deep planting.

Double blooming

To obtain a succession of blooms from daffodils or other
bulbs in containers, plant them in two layers, one about
5 cm below the other. The flowers from the deeper
planting will take longer to emerge than those from the
shallower one.

Propagating snowdrops

Transplant and divide snowdrops and aconites after the
flowers have faded but while they are still in full leaf –
they establish much better this way than as dry bulbs.

Storing dahlias

After lifting dahlias, use a short thin cane to poke out soil from between the individual tubers and stand the clump upside-down for a week before storing it.

Store dried dahlia tubers in a frost-free place in large envelopes, each made from an entire newspaper.

Planting irises

Plant rhizomatous irises very shallowly – only half bury the rhizomes, using your hands rather than a trowel or other tool to ensure that the roots are covered.

Crown imperials

Plant crown imperial bulbs on their sides to prevent water collecting round the crown and causing decay.

Planting begonias

Always plant tuberous begonias with the tuber hollow side up.

Crocuses

For a delightful purple crocus that will reliably bloom in the garden around Christmas time, choose *Crocus laevigatus fontenayi*.

When buying small species' bulbs and corms such as snowdrops, crocuses and cyclamen, look for a note on the packet that the plants have been raised in cultivation and not collected from the wild.

Early in the year, lift a clump of crocuses, pot them up and bring them indoors to provide some premature spring colour in the house.

To protect crocus corms from mice and voles which love to dig them up, lay fine mesh heavy duty plastic or chicken wire about 1 cm (⅓ in) above them when planting. The wire will of course be invisibly buried while the crocus shoots can emerge safely through it.

Gladioli

When lifting gladioli, carefully pull away the baby cormlets, store them separately and then pot them up in the spring. Keep them in pots for a couple of years by when, with liquid feeding, they should be large enough to plant out in the garden.

Do not plant all of your anemone and gladiolus corms at the same time: plant a few at a time over a period of a few weeks to give a succession of blooms.

Allow 100 days between planting gladiolus corms and the time you want the flowers.

If the tall, large-flowered gladioli are not entirely to your taste, try the smaller and more delicately bloomed butterfly varieties – especially the unusually coloured 'Greenland'.

Lily compost

Mix potting compost with an equal volume of leaf mould to make an ideal medium for growing lilies, and give the plants a top dressing of leaf mould and bonemeal every year.

Hyacinths

To be certain of having a uniform bowl of hyacinths, buy slightly more bulbs than you actually require and raise each separately in a 10 cm (4 in) pot. Then choose the most uniform group and arrange them, still in their pots, in the bowl and pack them round with bulb fibre.

After indoor hyacinths have finished flowering, cut off the old flower spike, give the plants liquid fertilizer and then, when the foliage dies down, lift and store the bulbs until the autumn when they can be planted in the garden.

Use sprigs of winter flowering shrubs such as forsythia to give support to the blooms of hyacinths growing in bowls – but take care to avoid unpleasant colour clashes.

Tulips

After lifting tulip or other bulbs for storage, allow them to dry briefly – but never in direct sun, which can cause serious damage.

After tulips have finished flowering, lift the plants carefully and replant them temporarily in an inconspicuous part of the garden until the foliage has died down. It yellows most unattractively and can spoil the appearance of an ornamental border.

Ornamental onions

For summer-flowering bulbs that are slightly different, try some of the species and varieties of ornamental onion, the alliums.

Orchids

Relatively few types of orchid make successful garden plants but among the terrestrial forms well worth growing, and readily obtainable, are the relatively hardy species of *Pleione*.

26

The rock garden and alpines

Natural rock garden

When constructing a rock garden, use only rock of a type that occurs locally – anything else will look peculiar; and arrange the rocks in the planes in which they were bedded naturally.

Table bed for alpines

For the simplest way of growing alpines, construct a table bed – a small, raised bed, confined by walls and containing very gritty, free-draining compost.

Shade tolerant

Easy-to-grow shade-tolerant alpines are not particularly common, but for a dark corner of the alpine bed, you will find the pretty little clump-forming *Oxalis adenophylla* generally successful.

Frost-free rock garden

Prop a sheet of glass over the buds of early-flowering rock garden plants to protect them from frost damage.

Alkaline gentian

Most gentians prefer an acid soil but *Gentiana septemfida* is the easiest of those that will succeed in alkaline conditions.

Alpine seed-sowing

Sow seed of gentians and other alpines in late autumn and leave the seed pans outdoors over winter when the frost and winter cold will break the seeds' dormancy.

Avoid snow-in-summer

Cerastium tomentosum, snow-in-summer, is often sold as an attractive rock garden plant. Resist the temptation to buy it for it is notoriously invasive and will soon become a problematic weed.

Successful lewisias

The secret of success with alpine lewisias is to plant them on a well-drained sloping surface (within crevices on a vertical face is ideal), for they are very prone to rot when water accumulates on the crowns.

Untidy alpine

An alpine bed should be neat and tidy in appearance and most alpine garden plants are clump-forming. A notable exception, and one to be avoided for this reason, is the rampant blue-flowered *Campanula portenschlagiana*.

Join the club

The growing of alpine plants encompasses such a wide range of species, many of which require rather distinct treatment, that you will find it well worthwhile to join a specialist alpine society and make contact with experts in the field.

Alpine trees

Although most alpines are herbaceous perennials, there are a few genuinely dwarf trees that can be included in your collection, one of the most appealing and easily obtainable being the tiny willow *Salix × boydii*.

Alpine fertilizer

A good general fertilizer for all alpine plants is supplied by a light general dressing of bonemeal in the early spring; this will provide phosphate for root growth and a small amount of nitrogen for foliar and shoot development.

Grit

Alpine plants, whether in rockery beds or in an alpine trough, should always have a little grit scattered round them. This is not only to enhance their appearance and help drainage, it is also to ensure that the flowers are not damaged by having soil splashed on to them by rain.

Alpines in the greenhouse

When growing alpine plants in a greenhouse, you will need no artificial heating and as much ventilation as possible – think of the alpine house as a large, well-aerated cloche.

Green carpet

To provide a tiny, soft green carpet that wraps itself over rocks and grit, grow one of the several species of *Raoulia*.

Saxifrage

A beginner to alpine gardening can do no better than select a range of species of saxifrage, a huge group of plants, very many of them relatively simple to grow and which are reliable in flowering.

Leave rocks alone

Never collect rocks and stones from the countryside for making your alpine garden. It is both illegal and environmentally vandalous. Rock of many different types is now readily available from garden centres.

High humidity

In fairly mild areas where the relative humidity is usually high (near the sea, for instance) you will find it harder to succeed with alpine plants that have woolly leaves, as these tend to attract the damp and rot very quickly.

27

House plants

Repotting

When repotting house plants, only do so into pots one size larger than the originals – and always take the opportunity to move the plants into clay rather than plastic pots.

Bedding plants

At the end of the summer, pot up a few bedding plants instead of throwing them all away – they make very pretty house plants for the winter.

Frost-free house plants

Move house plants into the room from windowsills at night in the winter – cold air from the window pane is trapped behind curtains and can cause damage.

Dwarf pot chrysanthemums

Don't try planting out dwarf pot chrysanthemums bought as house plants or keeping them after flowering has finished. They have been artificially dwarfed and make useless plants thereafter.

Azaleas

Take indoor azaleas outside for the summer at the time you turn off your central heating; and bring them in again when you turn it back on.

Never allow the roots of indoor pot azaleas to dry out – this is the commonest cause of them failing.

Coleus

Grow mixed coleus from seed in order to obtain a very inexpensive and attractive supply of ornamental house plants to give as gifts.

Perfumed wax plant

For an attractive house plant that is tolerant of dryness, semi-shade and a fair amount of neglect, yet also produces exquisitely perfumed flowers, try growing *Hoya carnosa*, the wax plant.

Cactus

Don't disturb a Christmas or Easter cactus plant while it is in full bud as this is likely to cause the buds to drop.

Succulent plants, especially species of cacti, should be given little or no water during the winter. Watering should begin gradually in the spring and a little liquid house plant fertilizer may then also be given.

Once-only poinsettia

Don't be tempted to try and induce a poinsettia to form its red bracts for a second year. It is very difficult to achieve without special equipment for careful regulation of day length. Keep it by all means, but as a normal, green foliage plant.

Spineless yucca

Snip the spines from the end of yucca leaves – some species have very vicious and dangerous spines that detract from their value as house plants. Cutting off the spines will do no harm to the plant.

Trial and error

Don't take too literally the advice given on labels and in specialist house plant books regarding the precise conditions in which different types of house plant should be grown. In my experience, you will generally fare better by moving the plants from place to place, leaving them for two or three weeks in each position and then deciding, by their growth and performance, which they most prefer.

Never in a terrarium

Never put flowering plants or those with very woolly leaves into a bottle garden or terrarium as they will very soon rot and spread mould to other plants too.

Wrap up warm

Always wrap a newly purchased house plant carefully in order to carry it home, especially in cold winter weather. Many potential Christmas presents deteriorate during a short, unprotected journey from garden centre to bus or car.

Choose colours with care

Be careful when choosing flowering house plants to select colours that will blend with those of your home decor; and don't use brightly coloured containers of clashing colour.

Pot-bound

If roots begin to appear through the drainage hole at the base of a plant pot, this is a sure indication that the plant is becoming pot-bound and should be re-potted into a container one size larger, preferably in the spring.

Separate arrangements

Quite frequently, shops sell so-called 'arrangements' in which several different house plants are grown in the same container. They may look attractive but usually some of the plants require different conditions or grow at different rates from the others. After the initial flush of appeal, therefore, they are better re-potted into individual containers.

Giants wanted

If you have a very large house plant that has outgrown its allotted space, don't try chopping it back or throwing it out. Very large specimens are rather valuable and are often sought after for offices or similar premises and you may know someone who will buy it from you.

Air plant

If you really have no time at all to look after house plants but would still like to share your home with something living, why not grow an air plant? These are species of *Tillandsia* that obtain both nutrient and moisture from the air. They are sold stuck on to some form of support – quite commonly a sea-shell, although they look much more attractive on a piece of bark.

Pot primulas

Many of the types of pot primula sold as house plants can be planted out in the garden after their flowering period is over where they will continue to give pleasure for many years. Check with the label that yours is not one of the tender kinds, but otherwise those that have the appearance of brightly coloured primroses are likely to fare best.

A very easy house plant

One of the easiest to grow of indoor foliage plants is the trailing, rather fleshy Swedish ivy, *Plectranthus*. It has lush, rich green foliage and, as an added bonus, strikes more readily from cuttings than any other plant I know.

28

Vegetables

Ground clearing

When starting a new vegetable garden, the most useful crop to plant first is potatoes although if the site was previously grassland, you must expect some damage from wireworms. Potatoes are effective at clearing the land of weeds by virtue of their dense cover and because of the amount of soil disturbance during hoeing and other aspects of their cultivation. Their extensive root systems also help improve soil structure.

Beneficial stones

Don't go to too much trouble in trying to remove stones from your vegetable garden soil: pebbles convey a positive benefit in retaining heat.

Catch crops

To make the best use of your kitchen garden space, grow fast-growing radishes or lettuces as catch crops – sow them where the rows of larger and more slowly maturing crops have been lifted, or in the gaps between rows of peas.

Crop rotation

Try to work out a three-course rotation for your vegetable garden to ensure that the nutrient resources of the soil are used as fully as possible, that all of the soil takes its turn at being cultivated and that pest and disease activity is minimized. The three groups to be rotated are: root vegetables, legumes and brassicas.

Deep bed

The best labour-saving way of growing vegetables is on a deep bed. Double dig a bed about 1.2 m (4 ft) wide and as long as space permits and incorporate large volumes of organic matter. Thereafter, avoid walking on the bed when planting, feeding, cultivating or harvesting (use a brick and plank 'bridge' if it helps). In this way, soil compaction will be minimized and digging should only be necessary every five years or so.

Equal spacing

The most efficient way of growing most types of vegetable is to space them equidistantly, rather than in rows where there will be small gaps between the plants but wide spaces between the rows.

How many vegetables?

Think carefully before deciding how many vegetables of each type to plant. A great deal of water is lost through leaves and in a dry year a large brassica, for instance, simply acts like a wick drawing out valuable soil moisture. Every unnecessary plant can result, therefore, in the loss of many litres of precious water.

Space saving

If vegetable growing space is limited, choose cut-and-come-again varieties such as leaf lettuce, calabrese and spinach which will continue to crop from the same plant.

Flower harvest

Flowers that are intended essentially for cutting are best grown in the kitchen garden where their removal won't affect the rest of a display.

Edible windbreak

In exposed gardens with poor soil, try planting Jerusalem artichokes as a windbreak for the vegetable plot.

Asparagus

Grow asparagus plants in flat beds at a spacing between plants of 30 cm (1 ft) each way: not on ridges as traditionally suggested, unless the soil is very badly drained.

Don't plant an asparagus bed until you are sure that the soil has been well cleared of perennial weeds, especially couch. They will be very difficult to eradicate later.

Don't cut asparagus spears after early June or you will weaken the plants, but do give them liquid fertilizer throughout the summer.

Celeriac

For success with celeriac, care is needed in earthing up – draw soil away from the roots regularly from about three weeks after planting out, and pull away the lower leaves, and then, in the autumn, hoe soil back over the swollen crowns to protect them.

Broad beans

In limited space, you may be able to obtain a crop of an early broad bean variety (although not a dwarf variety like 'The Sutton') by sowing between main crop potato tubers. Place one bean between each pair of tubers and you will be able to crop and dispose of the beans before the potatoes have caught them up.

In a small garden, choose the fairly dwarf broad bean variety 'The Sutton' for spring sowing.

Sow a few extra broad beans at the end of each row and use the spare plants to make up gaps; this is especially useful with overwintering varieties such as 'Aquadulce', which are most likely to suffer some losses during the cold weather.

Pinch out the tops of broad bean plants to encourage strong growth, plenty of flowers and discourage black fly which feeds on the succulent tips.

French beans

Pick French beans before the seeds swell sufficiently to cause bulges in the pods.

For the finest flavoured French bean variety, choose 'The Prince'.

Runner beans

After planting runner beans (as opposed to sowing them directly in their cropping positions), it will be necessary to tie the shoots to the support canes to encourage them to climb.

Space runner bean plants singly at the base of each

cane with 15 cm (6 in) (not 30 cm (1 ft) as often recommended) between the plants and 60 cm (2 ft) between the rows to give maximum yields.

When training runner beans up a tent-style support, save on the cost of canes by using canes and string alternately.

Use an alternation of red-and-white-flowered runner bean varieties for an attractive kitchen garden display.

Lift a few runner bean plants in the autumn, store their roots in the same way as dahlia tubers, and plant them again in the spring to give a few succulent beans rather earlier than usual.

To help ensure a good set on the lower trusses of runner beans, mulch the plants thickly and ensure that the roots are copiously supplied with water.

Plant runner and French beans in the most sheltered part of the vegetable garden for they are particularly prone to suffering reduced yields in windy places.

Brassicas

Brassicas benefit from being planted deeply in order to establish strong enough root systems to support their large heads. Plant them with the soil up to the level of their basal leaves.

If you are anxious for your brassicas and vegetable crops to mature gradually over a long period of time, choose traditional open-pollinated instead of F_1 hybrid varieties.

In limited space, don't grow biennial purple-sprouting broccoli, which occupies the ground for a long time, but choose annual varieties of calabrese instead.

Cabbage

To avoid the common problem of bolting in Chinese cabbage, choose fast-growing varieties and delay sowing until after midsummer.

After harvesting cabbages, leave the stump in the ground and cut a cross in the top. This will encourage tasty green shoots to form, giving you more return for your labours.

Carrots

In general, root crops such as carrots or parsnips do not respond well to being transplanted, but in late seasons or on poor soils, it can be beneficial provided the plants are raised individually in pots and then planted out with minimal disturbance to the compost in the pot ball.

If all else fails, carrot fly attack can sometimes be avoided by not growing early varieties and by delaying the sowing of the maincrop until early July when the activity of adult egg-laying flies has declined.

When growing carrots and other root crops for exhibition, whether in the open ground, or more seriously in containers filled with specially prepared compost, remove the roots by flooding round them – it is easier to pull a carrot from a mud pool without damage than it is from firm soil.

Never make the mistake of sowing carrot seed too deeply: on a good soil, this is the commonest reason for difficulty with the crop. A 0.5 cm (¼ in) drill is plenty deep enough.

Don't use fresh manure just before sowing carrots for it will bring about fanging of the roots; six months before sowing is soon enough.

Sow carrot seed sparingly to minimize the need for thinning later: every disturbance of the foliage will help to attract the carrot fly. And whenever you *do* disturb the plants, always go over them with a watering can or hosepipe afterwards to dampen down the aroma.

Avoid growing carrots on soil containing stones, hard clods or fresh manure, as all of these will encourage fanged and misshapen roots.

Sow quick-growing early varieties of carrots, beetroot and other vegetables at the *end* of the season to obtain an extra crop before the autumn.

On rough or stony soils, grow round or stump-rooted varieties of carrot.

If you cover carrots or other root crops with straw to protect them in the ground, do not put on this cover until the weather really begins to turn cold. Otherwise, the plants may continue to grow beneath the cover and spoil.

Cucumbers

Cucumbers, marrows and pumpkins are very prone to rotting at the stem base. To lessen the chance of this, place an old, bottomless plastic pot over the seed when sowing. As the plant develops, this will form a collar round its stem, and when you apply water be sure that none is poured inside this protective ring.

When sowing cucumber, marrow or melon seeds, always place the seeds on their sides.

To avoid bitterness in greenhouse cucumbers, remove male flowers as they arise to prevent any pollination (the cause of the bitterness), or grow one of the modern all-female varieties.

Cauliflowers

Try planting summer cauliflowers at a spacing of 10 cm (4 in) between plants and 20 cm (8 in) between rows to encourage the development of individual portion-sized mini-heads.

To obtain success with cauliflowers, never allow their growth to be checked – raise each plant in a pot of compost, knock it very carefully from the pot without disturbing the roots when transplanting and never allow the plants to dry out.

If you have too many cauliflowers to use at the same time and don't want to freeze them, you can keep them fresh by hanging them upside-down in a cool place.

Celery

For the hardiest celery, well able to stand into February in most areas, choose the variety 'Giant Red' – in general, the redder the variety, the hardier it is.

For traditional celery flavour, grow trenched varieties and forget about self-blanching types.

Sweetcorn

If you have no greenhouse, slightly tender vegetables such as sweet corn may easily be started in the open ground by sowing the seed in pairs about a month before the danger of frost is past and placing a jam or coffee jar over each pair of seeds to act as a miniature cloche.

Always plant sweet corn in blocks rather than in rows to be sure of obtaining good wind pollination.

Check the ripeness of sweet corn by pressing your thumb into one of the grains: if it is ripe, a thick (not watery) whitish liquid will ooze out.

Courgettes

Where space is limited, use bush rather than trailing varieties of courgette or marrow – two plants will suffice for most families.

For an attractive alternative to green courgettes, try growing a golden variety such as 'Gold Rush'.

Pick baby marrows as courgettes when they are about 10 cm (4 in) long; even those varieties sold specifically as courgettes will grow to become full-sized marrows if left.

Leeks

When planting leeks, trim the root and leaf tips before dropping each plant into a 15 cm (6 in) deep hole, then fill the hole with water.

Sweet peppers

Harvest sweet peppers when they are green or red; the flavour doesn't improve with the colour change.

While you should only plant two tomato plants into each growing bag, you may grow three peppers or aubergines.

If you grow your tomatoes by ring culture, you should be able to find room to grow peppers and aubergines too by placing the tomato pots slightly further back on the bed and positioning a pepper or aubergine pot between them at the front.

Potatoes

In a small garden, don't waste space on main crop potatoes. Use your potato-growing area for early varieties which will give you those delicious new potatoes. In most cases they will also store perfectly well, at least until Christmas.

Don't be tempted to save your own potato tubers for replanting – they will inevitably have built up virus contamination and crop inadequately as a result. Always buy fresh certified seed tubers each year.

After lifting potatoes intended for storage, allow them to dry briefly before bagging them.

If you wish to store large quantities of potatoes, this may conveniently be done in a traditional clamp. Choose an area of well-drained soil, pile the potatoes on this, cover them with a layer of about 10 cm (4 in) of straw and then, over this, pile a similar thickness of soil.

Don't stop earthing up potatoes once the danger of frost has passed. It is important to earth them during the summer also to prevent the tubers being exposed to the light and so becoming green and poisonous.

Plant early potato varieties with two sprouts per tuber (rub out any excess), but plant maincrop tubers with as many sprouts as possible.

Always store potatoes in paper, not plastic sacks, and stack them against the north inside wall of a shed, garage or other frost-free store.

To obtain new potatoes at Christmas time, dig a few small tubers from the ground in July and plant them in large buckets or tubs of potting compost. Move them into the greenhouse once frosts start.

On heavy soils especially, plant potatoes with a trowel, not a dibber, which tends to smear the soil and make it harder for roots to penetrate.

Plant early potato tubers at spacings of 60 cm (2 ft) between rows and 30 cm (1 ft) between plants, but maincrop varieties at 75 cm (2½ ft) and 45 cm (1½ ft) respectively.

Rub off the shoots from stored potato tubers to prolong their storage life by several weeks.

When selecting seed potato tubers, you will achieve better results from using tubers of hen's-egg size than from buying larger ones and cutting them up.

Don't be fooled by the tomato-like appearance of the green fruits that sometimes appear on potato plants: potato fruits are extremely poisonous.

Hamburg parsley

For an unusual, dual-purpose plant with roots like parsnips, leaves like parsley and a greater tolerance of shade than almost any other vegetable, try Hamburg parsley. The variety 'Omega' is the one most often seen.

Parsnips

Don't be disappointed at poor germination of parsnip seed. It germinates with notorious difficulty and parsnips are the only garden vegetables for which statutory minimum germination percentages are not laid down.

Peas

Always use two hands to pick peas. The pods are attached firmly to their stalks and if you try to hold a basket in one hand and pick peas with the other, you will simply pull the plants out of the ground.

Dig in the roots of peas and beans in the autumn – the nitrogen contained in their root nodules won't then be wasted in the compost heap.

Don't apply any nitrogen fertilizer to pea crops; they are able to manufacture their own nitrogen and will produce masses of foliage but few flowers if they are over-dosed with it.

After sowing peas, place some lightweight small mesh netting over the row to protect them from birds.

Once the seedlings have emerged, the netting should be replaced with support twigs or a wide-mesh support net.

Give support to peas once the plants are about 5 cm (6 in) tall.

Alternatively, to avoid having to use two types of netting over pea crops (a fine net after sowing to keep off the birds and then wide-mesh netting later for support), use cloches for the early protection. These are much more easily removed and have the additional advantage of encouraging uniform, rapid emergence.

Onions

Don't use a weeding hoe between rows of onions or you will damage their shallow roots; weed carefully by hand.

To produce pips (tiny bulblets) of prized onion or leek strains for replanting, carefully shave off the flower buds from the flower head with a razor blade just before they open, but be sure to leave the tiny flower stalks in place. The pips will then form on the old flower head and can be harvested and planted like sets.

Small onion sets may cost more per unit weight than large ones, but they work out cheaper per plant – and the plants are less likely to bolt.

Sowing time is critical with overwintered Japanese onion varieties – at the beginning of August in the north of England and Scotland but not until a month later in the south of England.

Dust the seed of bulb onions with benomyl fungicide if they are being grown for storage: it will prevent the development of neck rot disease after they have been lifted.

Although you will sometimes succeed with normal 'White Lisbon' salad onions sown in the autumn, you will fare much better with seed of the special winter hardy variant.

When planting onion sets, shallots or garlic, never push the bulbs into the soil – use a trowel when planting them and, with garlic and shallots, be sure to leave a wisp of the shoot showing through the soil.

Radishes

To avoid the almost inevitable frustration of feeble plants or bolting, don't sow normal radish varieties after the end of June; winter radish can of course be sown in autumn.

Rhubarb

If flower spikes arise on rhubarb plants, pull them away promptly or they will weaken the plants.

Never pull more than a third of the stems from one rhubarb plant at a time as this will seriously weaken it.

Force a clump of rhubarb by placing an old bucket or similar vessel with a hole in the bottom over it – but don't force the same clump again for two years.

Shallots

In milder areas, plant shallots on the shortest day of the year (22 December) and harvest them on the longest (21 June); although in cold regions and cold seasons, it may be better to wait until February before planting.

Brussels sprouts

When harvesting Brussels sprouts, it is generally best to cut rather than pull the sprouts to avoid damaging the stem.

Stake Brussels sprout plants as soon as they are established – even in the least windy parts of the country, they are liable to work loose in the ground and crop badly in consequence. In very windy areas, select shorter growing varieties.

Remove yellowing leaves from Brussels sprout stems; they will be of no further use to the plant and can harbour pests and diseases.

Brussels sprouts should be harvested sequentially from the bottom of the stem, not from the top – the oldest, most mature sprouts are below the younger ones.

Spinach

Spinach is notorious for running to seed, especially in dry conditions and on light soils. If all else fails, try growing the slightly different New Zealand spinach which is most unlikely to bolt.

Watercress

Watercress need not be grown in water. Plant sprigs from a bunch into any area of soil that can be kept fairly damp and they will grow satisfactorily, although the more water you supply the less strong will be the flavour.

29

Tomatoes

Wilt disease

Don't grow tomatoes in soil beds in a greenhouse if you don't want to run the risk of them contracting wilt disease, which almost invariably builds up in soil after a few years of cropping.

Cold shock

Never plant tomatoes into cold soil as the shock causes a check to growth. If you are growing them in a greenhouse by one of the container methods such as pots or growing bags, bring the containers into the greenhouse about a week in advance in order to allow the compost to warm up.

Supports for growing bags

To support tomato plants in a growing bag, insert a vertical cane in the soil behind the bag (or peg one to the wall) and use a small diagonal cane from the hole in the bag to train the plant's stem up to the vertical.

Outdoor varieties

For outdoor use, choose bush rather than staked varieties of tomato: they are less labour intensive, requiring no regular tying in or side-shooting.

Yellow tomatoes

When choosing tomato varieties, don't forget the yellow-fruited types – they have excellent flavour and make an attractive alternative for salads.

Side-shooting

Always side-shoot tomatoes with finger and thumb: by using a knife or secateurs, you are more than likely to damage the main stem of the plant.

When side-shooting tomato plants, pay particular attention to the back of the plant as it is very easy to overlook shoots emerging from behind.

Encouraging fruit set

Tap greenhouse tomato plants round the hottest period of the day when they are in flower in order to encourage good fruit set.

How many trusses?

Pinch out the top of greenhouse tomato plants when they have six fruit trusses but allow only four or five trusses to develop on outdoor plants (other than bush varieties).

Fresh manure

Never use fresh strawy manure near to tomato plants – the straw may well contain weedkiller residues that can be very damaging to tomatoes.

Yellow leaves

Only pull off the lower leaves from tomato plants if they become yellowed or attacked by diseases or pests: the plant requires all of its healthy foliage to help produce good quality fruit.

Best variety

Easily the best flavoured tomato variety for greenhouse or outdoors is the small-fruited, heavy-cropping 'Gardeners' Delight' – and don't believe anyone who tells you otherwise.

Greenback

Be sure to supply shading to a greenhouse where tomatoes are being grown, as fruit close to the glass are likely to suffer from the imperfect ripening condition known as greenback.

Ring culture

If you are likely to be away from home a good deal and unable to attend to watering as frequently as you would wish, grow your tomatoes in ring culture pots (bottomless rings filled with compost and standing on a gravel bed) as they are much less likely to dry out with this method.

Beefsteak varieties

One of the biggest problems with most varieties of the large-fruited, beefsteak tomatoes is that the fruit split very easily. The most reliable in this respect (and one of the best flavoured) I have found to be 'Dombito'.

Feeding

Once the first fruit truss has set, feed greenhouse tomatoes twice a week and outdoor tomatoes once a week.

Blossom end rot

One of the commonest problems on tomatoes is blossom end rot, in which a dark lesion arises at the blossom end of the fruit. It is caused by a deficiency of calcium, exacerbated by water shortage and its effects can be minimized by ensuring that the compost never dries out.

Unhappy combination

Although tomatoes can be grown successfully in the same greenhouse as cucumbers, the combination is not ideal because while tomatoes require a fairly dry atmosphere, cucumbers prefer more moist conditions.

Green tomatoes

At the end of the season, there will still be plenty of green tomatoes left on the plant. The best way to harvest these is to cut off the whole plant and carefully hang it, upside-down, in a cool, well-ventilated place. As the tomatoes are required, they should be removed and brought into the warmth for ripening.

30

Herbs

Raised from cuttings

Almost all types of herb are better bought as plants of named varieties that have been raised from cuttings rather than from seeds.

Preserving parsley

If you don't have space to grow parsley and other herbs through the winter, the simplest way of preserving them is by freezing. Dried herbs are about as much use as sawdust.

Fennel

Fennel is both an attractive herb and an attractive foliage ornamental but it self-seeds wickedly. If you have the bronze form and want to keep a population of bronze plants, you will have to weed out all green seedlings.

Colourful salad

Use the edible flowers of nasturtiums to add a splash of colour to summer salads.

Garlic

Pot up a few garlic cloves in spring and keep them on the window sill or in the greenhouse to supply green shoots for flavouring.

When harvesting garlic, leave a 25–30 cm (8–12 in) length of dry stem attached to the roots. This will enable you to plait the stems together and so form an attractive and useful 'rope' for storage.

When buying garlic for planting in the garden, always try to obtain the Isle of Wight strain which has been specially selected as suitable for British conditions.

Mint

Plant a few mint runners in pots early in the New Year and bring them indoors to provide fresh young shoots to use with spring lamb.

Hold a sprig of eau de Cologne mint under your bath tap to give a delicious fragrance.

Grow mint in 25 cm (10 in) diameter plastic pots sunk to their rims in the ground. Lift the pots every autumn and trim off any shoots or runners that threaten to escape.

For the best mint sauce, use the woolly-leaved apple mint; for new potatoes, spearmint is better.

Thyme

For the best thyme to combine rich flavour with attractive appearance, choose the bushy 'Silver Posy'; many other varieties, including those raised from seed, have little if any flavour.

Borage

Use the rich blue flowers of borage to add interest to cold drinks – drop single fresh flowers into the water in each of the compartments of an ice cube tray. The flowers freeze in the cubes and float out into your drink when the ice melts.

Use rosemary to form a quick-growing and very attractive low dividing hedge for the kitchen garden.

A pot of basil

One of the most useful and delicious of all herbs is basil. It is also, unfortunately, one of the few that is not hardy in Britain. Grow it each year from seed but be sure to pot up a few plants for indoor use. By regularly pinching back the tops, you will produce bushy plants that will keep you well supplied through the winter.

Superior tarragon

Tarragon is delicious with chicken but when buying a plant be sure you select French Tarragon. It is sometimes possible to buy so-called Russian tarragon which is greatly inferior.

A short life

Almost all herbs become straggly and unkempt after a few years and shouldn't be considered as long-term plants. The herb bed is best renewed with fresh stock every four or five years therefore.

31

Tree fruit

Too high for fruit

You will be unlikely to grow tree fruit very satisfactorily in a garden more than about 175 m (600 ft) above sea level unless you provide them with protection.

Heavy branches

Erect a permanent wooden prop beneath the spreading branches of old plum and other fruit trees to prevent them from breaking under the weight of fruit.

Root pruning

Root pruning is sometimes recommended to increase the productivity of fruit trees but should never be performed on plums or damsons as it will encourage the development of suckers.

All-round pruning

When pruning fruit trees, always walk round the trees regularly to ensure that you are not cutting too much from one side and causing them to lose their shape.

Sunshine for peaches

Pull or temporarily peg back a few of the leaves on peach trees to ensure that the fruit are fully exposed to the sun.

Best value crab apple

For a crab apple to combine ornamental appeal with the best fruit, choose the white-flowered 'John Downie'.

Pest deterrent

One of the best ways of keeping fruit tree pests in check is to allow chickens to feed beneath the trees. They will unearth and eat all manner of insects and their larvae.

Harvesting apples

When harvesting apples for storage be sure not to pull out the stalk, and reject any fruit showing signs of damage or decay. Look particularly carefully at the eye and stalk ends for signs of the holes made by the codling moth – reject any fruit that are at all blemished.

Chopped apples for compost

Chop windfall apples with a spade (or put them through the shredder) before adding them to the compost heap. Left unbroken, they will not rot for months.

Is it ripe?

Check the ripeness of apples by gently lifting a fruit while it is still on the tree. When ripe, its stalk will detach itself from the branch.

Dual-purpose

Dual-purpose (eating and cooking) apple varieties such as 'Blenheim Orange' are well worth considering where space is a limiting factor.

Miniature apple trees

Where space is limited, grow apple varieties grafted on to the dwarfing rootstock M.27. They will never be taller than 2 m (6 ft) and are small enough to grow in containers, or for edging paths in the kitchen garden.

Apple trees grown on dwarfing rootstocks must be kept staked throughout their lives.

June drop

Don't be concerned when large numbers of immature fruit drop from your apple trees during early summer. This phenomenon is called the June drop and is simply the tree's way of ridding itself of those excess fruits that it will be unable to mature.

Spacing

Plant cordon apples 1 m (3 ft) apart but espaliers 4 m (15 ft) apart.

Storing apples and pears

Store apples separately from pears because the latter need checking regularly for ripeness while apples are best left undisturbed.

Storing apples

Store apples in tens or dozens in clean plastic bags, tied at the top but with a few ventilation holes punctured in the sides, and then lay them on slatted shelves in a cool place.

Compatible trees

When selecting apple trees, check that you have compatible varieties – all apples require pollen from another variety in order to produce fruit, and some common ones such as 'Bramley's Seedling' actually need two others.

All pear varieties require another variety planted nearby to aid pollination; even those that are partially self-fertile such as 'Conference' will crop better with a pollinator variety. This is not true of self-fertile plum varieties such as 'Victoria' and 'Czar', however, which will give very good crops from an isolated tree.

Space-saving apples

Where space is limited, buy a family apple tree on which several varieties have been grafted on to the same rootstock, or grow your trees as cordons or espaliers.

Fruit trees on walls

In exposed areas, plant pear and plum trees against walls to provide protection and encourage fruiting.

Which apple?

When selecting rootstocks for apple trees, remember that the more dwarfing the rootstock, the better the growing conditions it needs; and the more vigorous the variety, the more dwarfing the rootstock needed to restrict it.

Before selecting apple varieties for your garden, try to sample those growing in neighbours' gardens (after first asking the neighbours) or visit a local pick-your-own fruit farm. The same varieties grown in different areas and on different soils can vary widely in taste.

Walnut

When buying a walnut, be sure to purchase from an experienced fruit nursery and to choose a plant taken as a graft from a tree known to produce abundant crops – many walnut trees are all but sterile even when fully grown.

Productive north wall

For a productive plant on a north wall, try the Morello cherry, trained in a fan pattern.

Peach and apricot

Help peach and apricot trees to set fruit by dusting the blossoms with a fluffy brush – they flower early in the year (apricots especially so) when few insects are active.

Figs

Unlike all other types of fruit, a fig should be starved. Confine its roots within a 1 m (3 ft) cube planting hole using concrete slabs as sides and filled with rubble.

The best fig variety for garden cultivation is 'Brown Turkey'.

Best plum

The best all-round plum variety for cooking and eating is 'Victoria', which has the additional merit of being self-fertile.

Cherry

Because birds are so fond of cherries, it is difficult to grow them successfully in gardens. The best plan for sweet cherries is to choose the self-fertile variety 'Stella' grafted on the dwarfing rootstock 'Colt'. This makes a tree small enough to be grown in a reasonably sized fruit cage.

When to prune

Free-standing (as opposed to cordon- or espalier-trained) apple trees need only be pruned in the winter. There are too many other important things to do with your time in the summer.

Lime shortage

Fruit malformation and poor stone development in plums, cherries, peaches and other stone fruits is very often due to a shortage of lime in the soil.

Propagating peaches

Almost alone among fruit trees, good fruiting peaches can often be grown by planting a stone – very few other types come true from seed.

Fruit inspection

Check over stored fruit regularly and remove any showing signs of decay – the disease may spread to sound fruit in contact.

Fruit in difficult conditions

One of the most successful tree fruit in cold, windy or otherwise difficult conditions is the damson. It makes an excellent choice for planting in a traditional mixed hedge. For the largest and most juicy fruit, choose the variety 'Merryweather'.

Apricots

If you are able to provide even a small amount of shelter in your garden try planting an apricot. They are much less tender than is generally imagined and, being self-fertile, will produce a crop from a single tree.

32

Soft fruit

Fruit-cage

In most parts of the country, soft fruit must be grown in a cage to give them protection from birds. Although you can buy purpose-made cages, they are fairly expensive and you can make your own very simply with some stout posts and a roll or two of netting.

Check fruit-cage netting at the beginning of winter to be sure that there are no gaps or holes through which bullfinches and other fruit-eating birds could enter.

Don't use galvanized wire as the roof of a fruit-cage or over strawberry plants; zinc, washed from the wire by rain, will be damaging. Use a plastic net instead.

Grapes

The best all-round grape variety for greenhouse cultivation in our climate is 'Black Hamburgh'.

Success with grapevines depends on supplying copious amounts of water, especially during the fruiting season.

Don't be too greedy with grapevines. Thin out the side-shoots to leave one for every 45 cm (18 in) of rod length; then remove flower trusses to leave one for every 30 cm (1 ft) of side-shoot and thin out the tiny grapes within the bunches, carefully removing approximately half of them with scissors.

Strawberries

The best flavoured strawberry is still the old variety 'Royal Sovereign', although it is not high yielding and the plants are best renewed after one or two years.

Cut off strawberry runners as they form – it is a false economy to root them as they will almost certainly be contaminated with virus; always buy new plants.

For a few small but tasty strawberry fruits over a very long period, try the Alpine variety 'Baron Solemacher'.

Raspberries

When pruning summer-fruiting raspberries, cut out the old canes to soil level immediately after they have fruited. Tie in the new canes at the same time.

Don't prune autumn-fruiting raspberries until February; then cut *all* canes back to soil level.

When pruning raspberries, don't leave more than seven canes per plant – cut out the weaker ones or those farthest from the training wires.

When planting raspberry canes, plant several canes in a row in a trench rather than placing each in an individual hole – and be sure that the uppermost roots are no deeper than 5 cm (2 in) below the soil surface.

In a small garden grow two or three raspberry plants round a central post rather than arranging them in lines.

Use hoes and other cultivation tools with care when working close to raspberry canes, which are shallowly rooted. Damage to the roots can encourage suckering.

Blackberries

The easiest system for training blackberries and similar fruits is to tie in the shoots to their support wires in a fan pattern – re-tie last season's canes towards the outer part of the fan early in the year and tie in the new season's canes in the gap that has been vacated in the centre.

Many of the old varieties of blackberry are too vigorous for garden use, while many others never produce fruit that matches the wild blackberry in flavour. A relatively new variety called 'Ashton Cross', however, is not too vigorous and, being a selection of the wild plant, has the best flavour of any cultivated variety I have tried.

Loganberries

The loganberry is a delicious summer fruit and the best variety for gardens is the thornless form called 'LY 654'.

Alternative to raspberries

For fruit with delicious flavour, similar to raspberries but larger, try growing the Tayberry.

Plant blackcurrants deep

Plant blackcurrant bushes several centimetres (2 or 3 in) deeper than the soil mark on the stem base to encourage the formation of new shoots.

Picking currants

When picking red, black or white currants, you will avoid squashing them if you pull off the strigs (fruit

176

bunches) entire and then strip off the individual fruits later in the kitchen.

Blueberries

If your garden has very acid soil try growing blueberries. The fruit is delicious and their leaves have the added advantage of displaying wonderful autumn colours. They are however fairly large plants and you will succeed best if you have two separate varieties to aid pollination – 'Bluecrop' should be one of them.

Worcesterberries

As an interesting alternative to gooseberries, try the dark-fruited Worcesterberry. Their cultivation is the same but as they are even more densely prickly, they are best managed when grown as cordons.

Spacing

On heavy soils or shaded sites, space gooseberry and blackcurrant bushes about 25 per cent wider apart than normally recommended to improve air circulation and lessen the chances of mildew attack.

Buy new plants

Don't bother to take cuttings from soft fruit canes and bushes: old stock will almost certainly be contaminated with virus and it is more sensible to buy fresh certified plants.

Pretty and sweet

One of the prettiest cane fruit, and one that also has an interesting flavour, is the orange-fruited Japanese wine berry, *Rubus phoenicolasius*.

Standard gooseberries

It is sometimes possible to obtain gooseberry bushes in which the plants have been grafted on to the top of a tall stem, thereby creating a standard and rendering the fruit very much easier to pick.

Easier picking

Redcurrants, white currants and gooseberries will be very much easier to pick if they are grown as cordons, trained against horizontal wires.

Index

irrigation systems 26
irritant sap 35
ivy 107, 110

Japanese anemones 122, 132
Japanese maples 104
Japanese onions 157
Japanese wine berries 178
jasmine, winter 110
Jekyll, Gertrude 118
Jerusalem artichokes 148
John Innes potting compost
    22
June drop 169

kniphofias 121
knives, pruning 62

laburnum 35
ladders 33
Lathyrus grandiflorus 120
    L. latifolius 120
laurel 69, 106
Lavatera 'Silver Cup' 128
lavender 69, 119
lawn mowings 28, 43, 50
lawnmowers 20, 30, 49, 75,
    94–5, 96
lawns 49–50, 93–9
layering 56
lead-free petrol 30
leaf bud cuttings 55
leaf mould cages 21
leafy cuttings 53
leatherjackets 41

leaves:
    clearing up in autumn 9
    removing from ponds 86
    silver 122
    woolly 140, 143
leeks 154, 157
legumes 147
lettuces 146, 148
lewisias 138
lichens 9
light, greenhouses 80
lighting, outdoor 7
Ligularia 121
lilacs 110
lilies 55, 135
Lilium candidum 133
lily of the valley 132
lime 12, 21, 43, 172
limestone 12, 22
linings, ponds 85
liquid fertilizers 16, 26, 54, 86
'living mulch' 114–15
loam 11, 46, 98
lobelia 59, 60, 126, 127
loganberries 176
loppers 62
lupin aphids 121
lupins 121

Madonna lilies 133
magnifiers 5
magnolias 105
mail order 105
maintenance 9–10
Mammillaria 35
manure 12, 14, 15, 16, 23, 70,
    86, 151–2, 162
maples, Japanese 104

Dr Stefan Buczacki
The Essential Gardener £25.00
A Personal Guide to Successful Modern Gardening

What are the priorities of today's gardeners? We are aware of the importance of environmental conservation, interested in encouraging wildlife and wild plants, and reluctant to use many chemicals. We are curious to grow new varieties of plants, especially fruit and vegetables, but also to rediscover neglected ones. We don't want to spend a great deal of money on plants and materials. We wish to spend less time working in the garden, and more time relaxing in it.

Stefan Buczacki, one of Britain's most popular and authoritative gardening experts, has written *The Essential Gardener* to meet these new requirements. Discarding the outdated and irrelevant information which appears in many general books, he has included here all the essentials of modern gardening practice. You won't find here the details of how to carry out bridge-grafting, but you will find clear, practical advice based on the author's long experience of how to plan, stock and maintain a beautiful and productive 'green' garden.
Published by Sidgwick & Jackson

Roger Phillips and Nicky Foy
Herbs £17.50

An indispensable new reference book for every herb enthusiast

Herbs follows Roger Phillips' other innovative natural history books in providing the most beautifully illustrated guide to the subject yet available.

Colour photographs of over 400 herbs from all over the world are accompanied by text describing their myriad uses in cooking, cosmetics and medicine.

Organized in nine sections – culinary herbs, salad herbs, vegetables, berries, teas, scented herbs, strewing herbs, dyeing herbs and medicinal herbs – the plants are arranged as far as possible in order of flowering.

Botanical details such as where the plant may be found, hints on how to plant and cultivate a herb garden, the traditional and modern medicinal uses, the preparation of infusions and any warning on the dangers inherent in each plant are all found in the accompanying text.

Roger Phillips and Martyn Rix
Perennials
(2 volumes) £17.50 each

Perennials is the definitive new two-volume reference book in the beautiful Pan Garden Plants series by Roger Phillips and Martyn Rix.

Perennials are plants that flourish from year to year in temperate climates, but die down to the ground in the winter. They are also known as 'herbaceous perennials'.

Volume One: Early Perennials covers plants that flower in the spring and early summer, including such favourites as Helleborus, Euphorbia, Viola, Peonia, Geranium and Iris.

Volume Two: Late Perennials includes, among others, Hosta, Day lily, Aster, Red Hot Poker, Delphinium, Astilbe, Phlox and Campanula, as well as ground covering, water and waterside plants, ferns and an extensive list of nurseries and gardens to visit.

In both volumes, colour photographs of over 1,250 perennials from around the world, both wild and cultivated, are accompanied by authoritative text describing their origins, characteristics, frost hardiness and favoured growing conditions.

Nicola Ferguson
Right Plant, Right Place £10.99

The indispensable guide to the successful garden

The unique reference book that will lead gardeners quickly and easily to the plants that will look best and grow best in their own particular gardens. Over 1,400 garden plants, all illustrated in full colour, are systematically organized according to growing conditions, purpose and appearance.

Right Plant, Right Place compresses a shelf full of reference books and a pile of seed catalogues into a single comprehensive guide to choosing plants.

All Pan books are available at your local bookshop or newsagent, or can be ordered direct from the publisher. Indicate the number of copies required and fill in the form below.

Send to: **CS Department, Pan Books Ltd., P.O. Box 40,**
            Basingstoke, Hants.   RG21 2YT.

or phone: 0256 469551 (Ansaphone), quoting title, author
            and Credit Card number.

Please enclose a remittance* to the value of the cover price plus: 60p for the first book plus 30p per copy for each additional book ordered to a maximum charge of £2.40 to cover postage and packing.

*Payment may be made in sterling by UK personal cheque, postal order, sterling draft or international money order, made payable to Pan Books Ltd.

Alternatively by Barclaycard/Access:

Card No.

Signature:

Applicable only in the UK and Republic of Ireland.

While every effort is made to keep prices low, it is sometimes necessary to increase prices at short notice. Pan Books reserve the right to show on covers and charge new retail prices which may differ from those advertised in the text or elsewhere.

NAME AND ADDRESS IN BLOCK LETTERS PLEASE:

....

Name

Address

3/87